Creatures of the
DEEP & WILD
— Adult Coloring Book —

Author and Illustrator: Annarine Chapman

Anne's Illustrations and Rustic Art

Colorist Leopard *(front cover)*: Dawn Jones

Colouring books have become a wonderful way of destressing and tapping into ones inner child. I hope that you enjoy my book as much as I have enjoyed designing it.

'Creatures of the wild and deep' is my second adult colouring book. I love both sea creatures and wild animals. With creating this book I am hoping that you will see how special and enjoyable it can be.

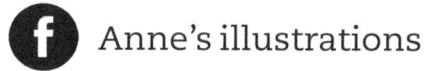 Anne's illustrations   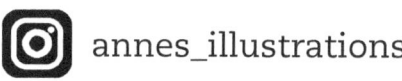 annes_illustrations

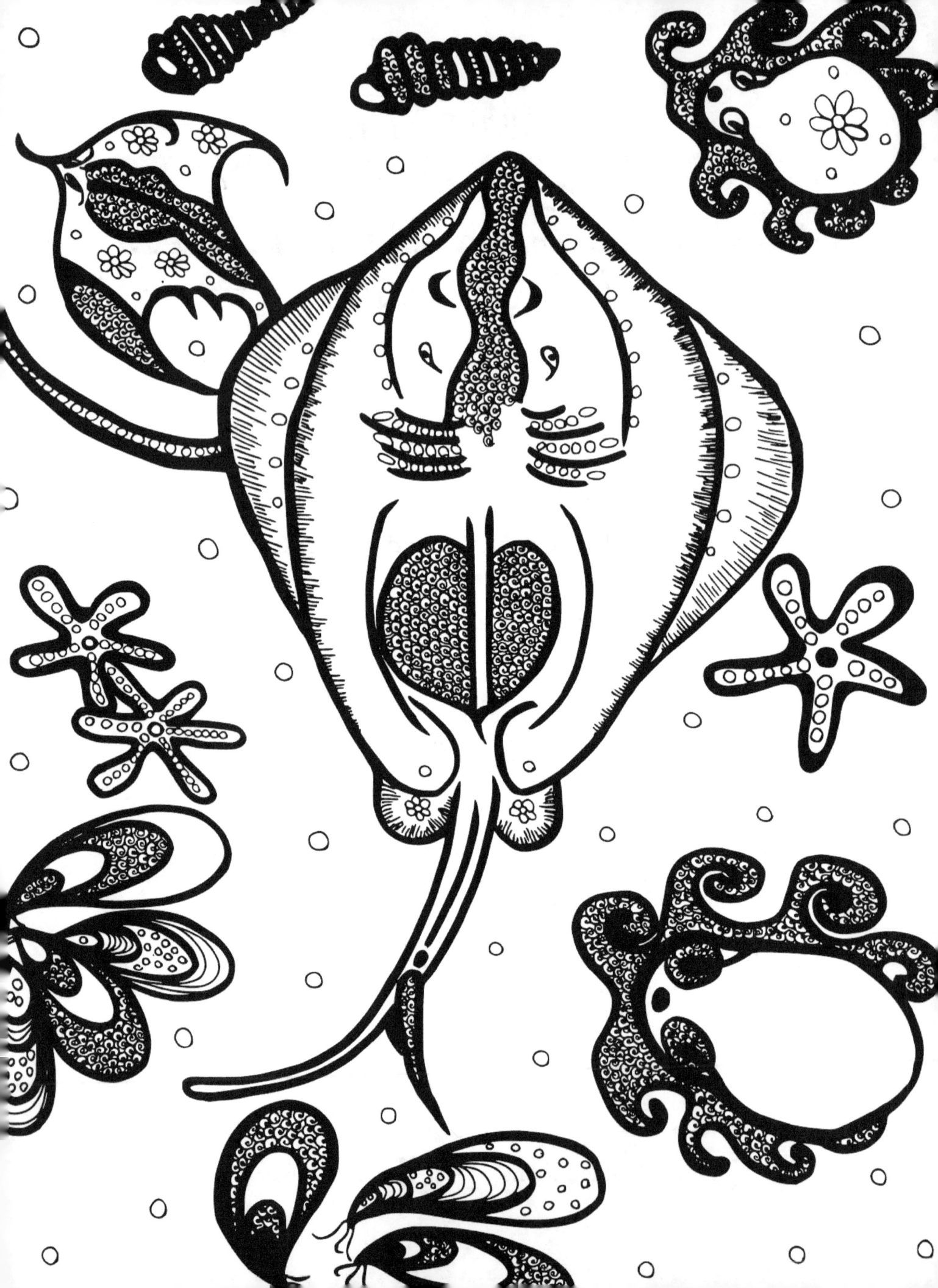

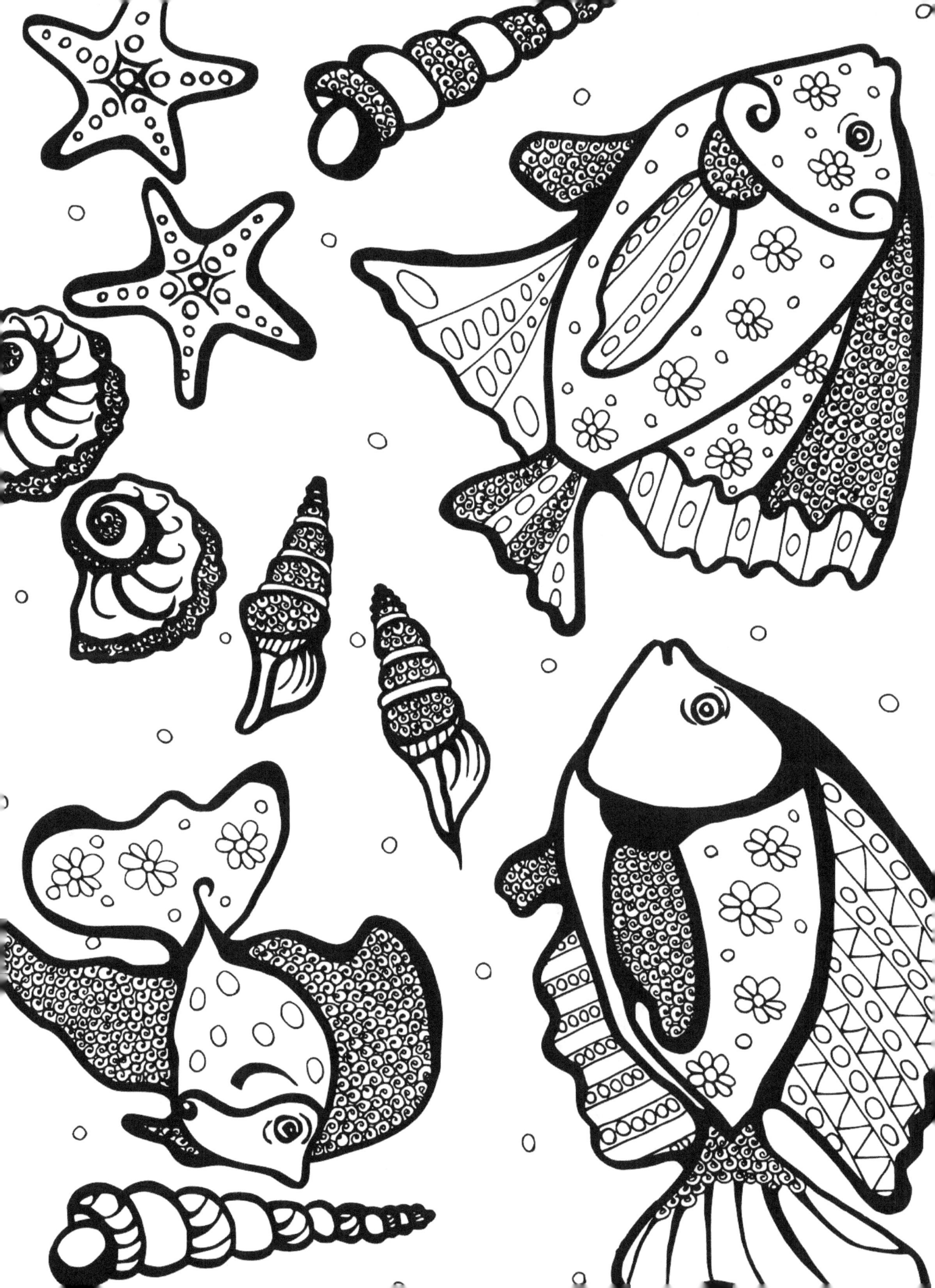

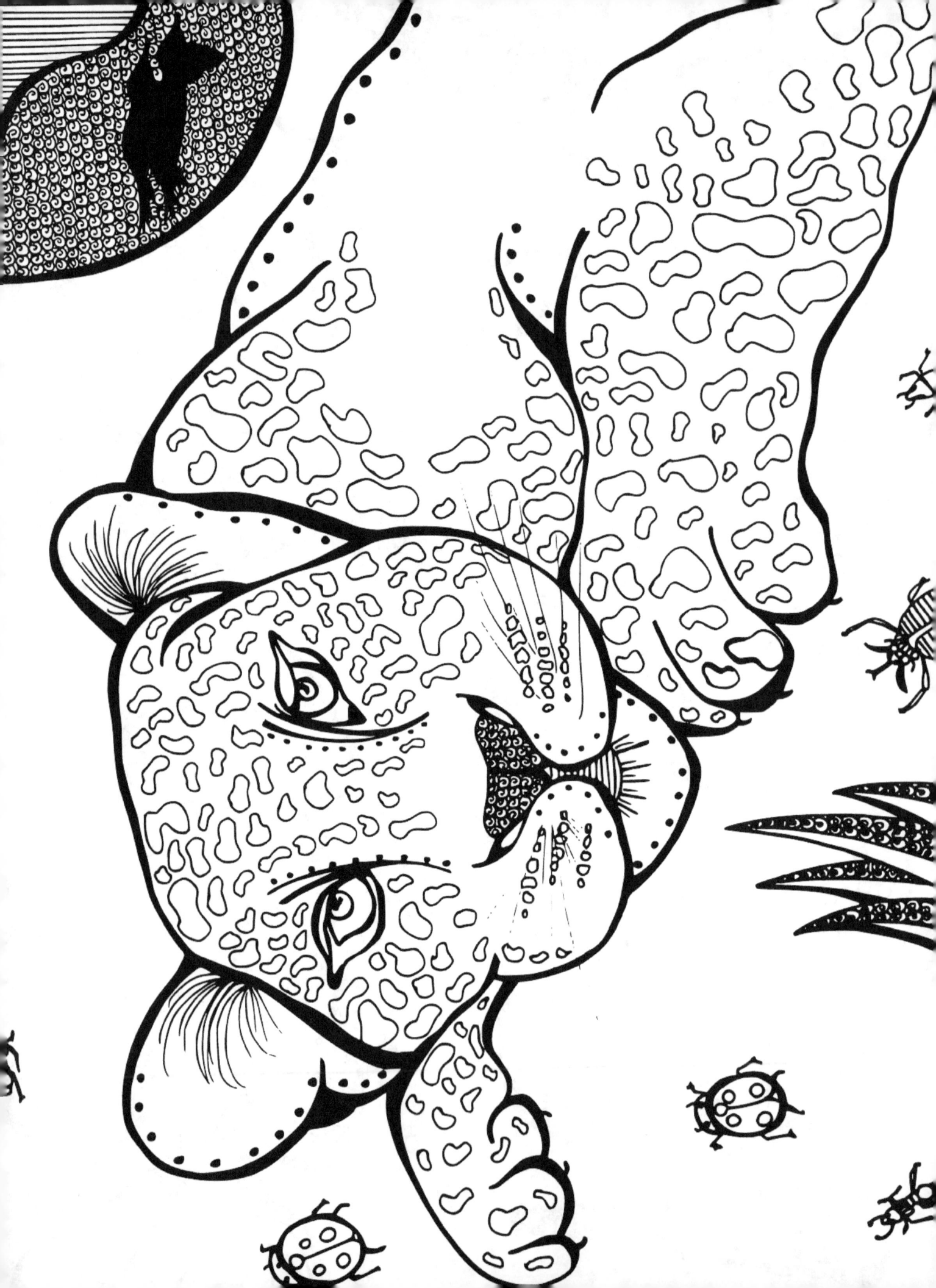

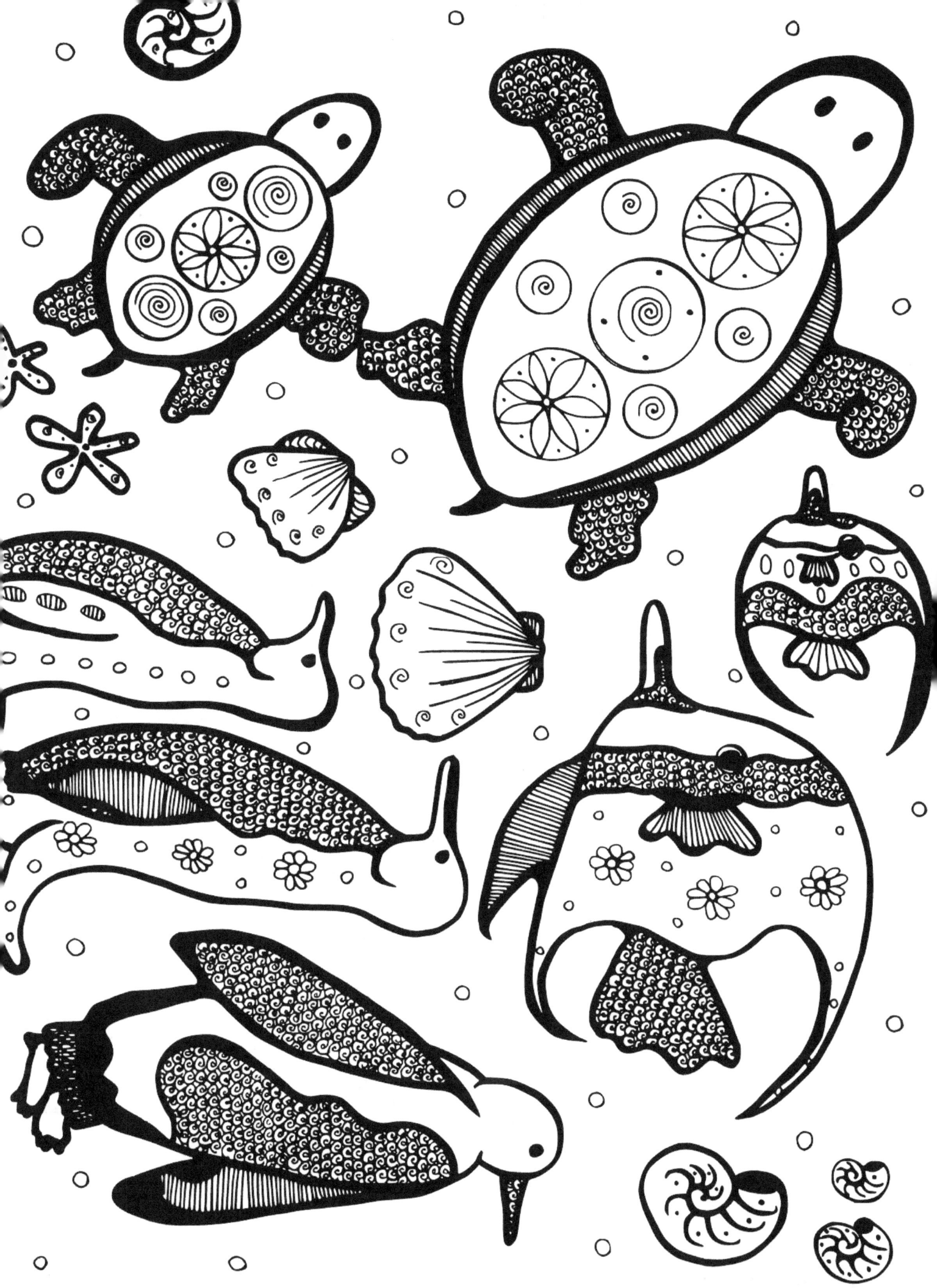

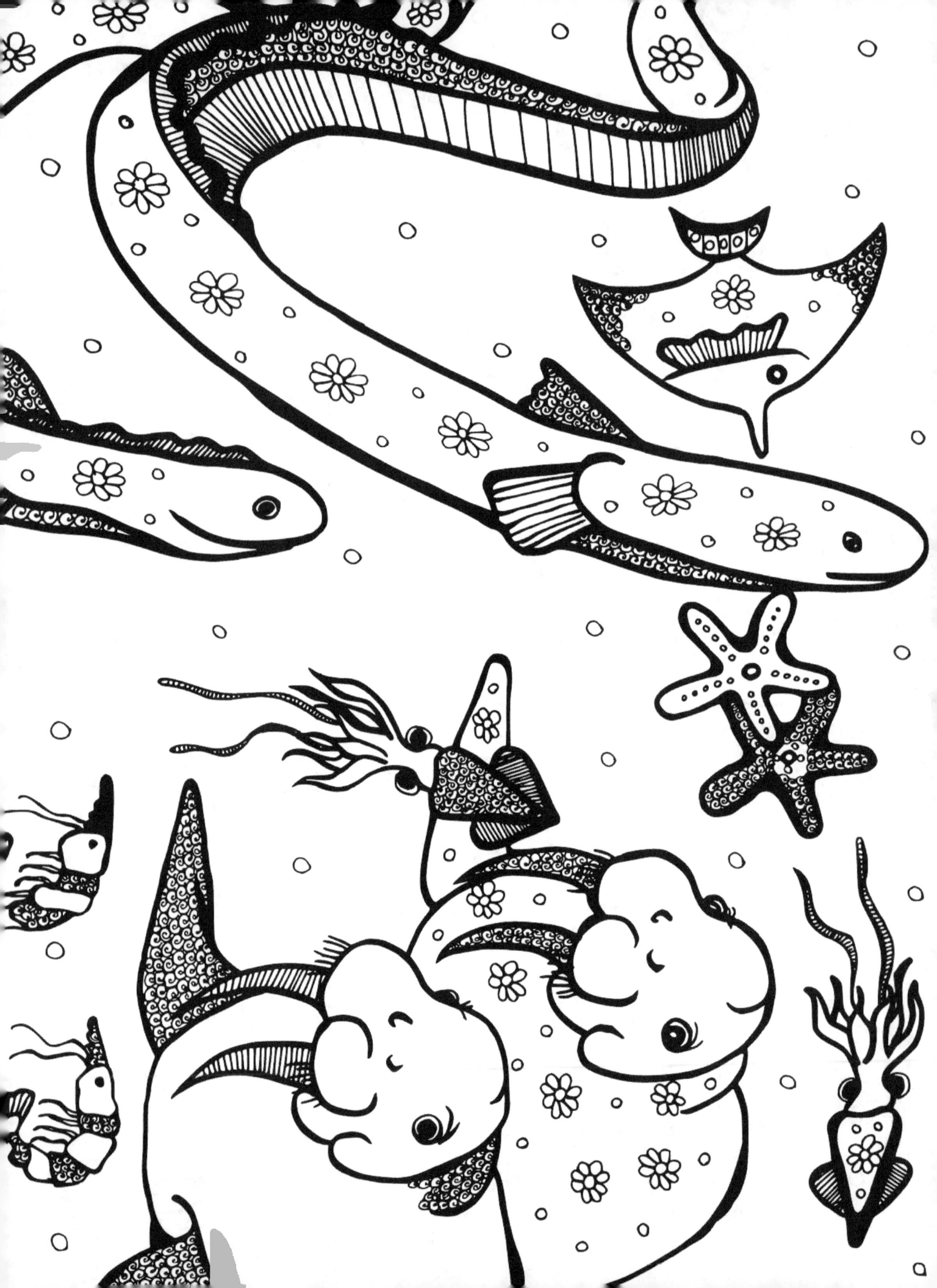

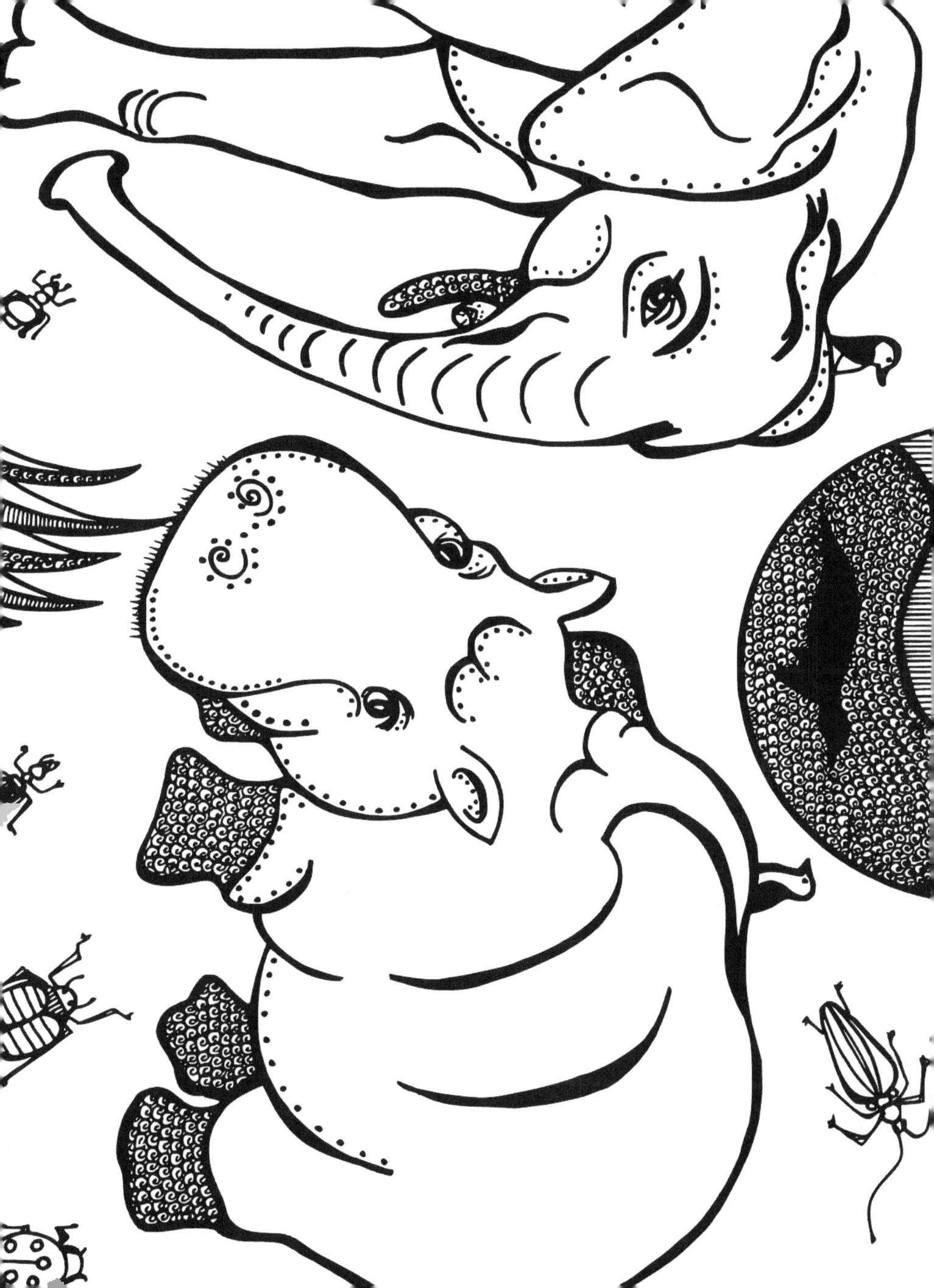

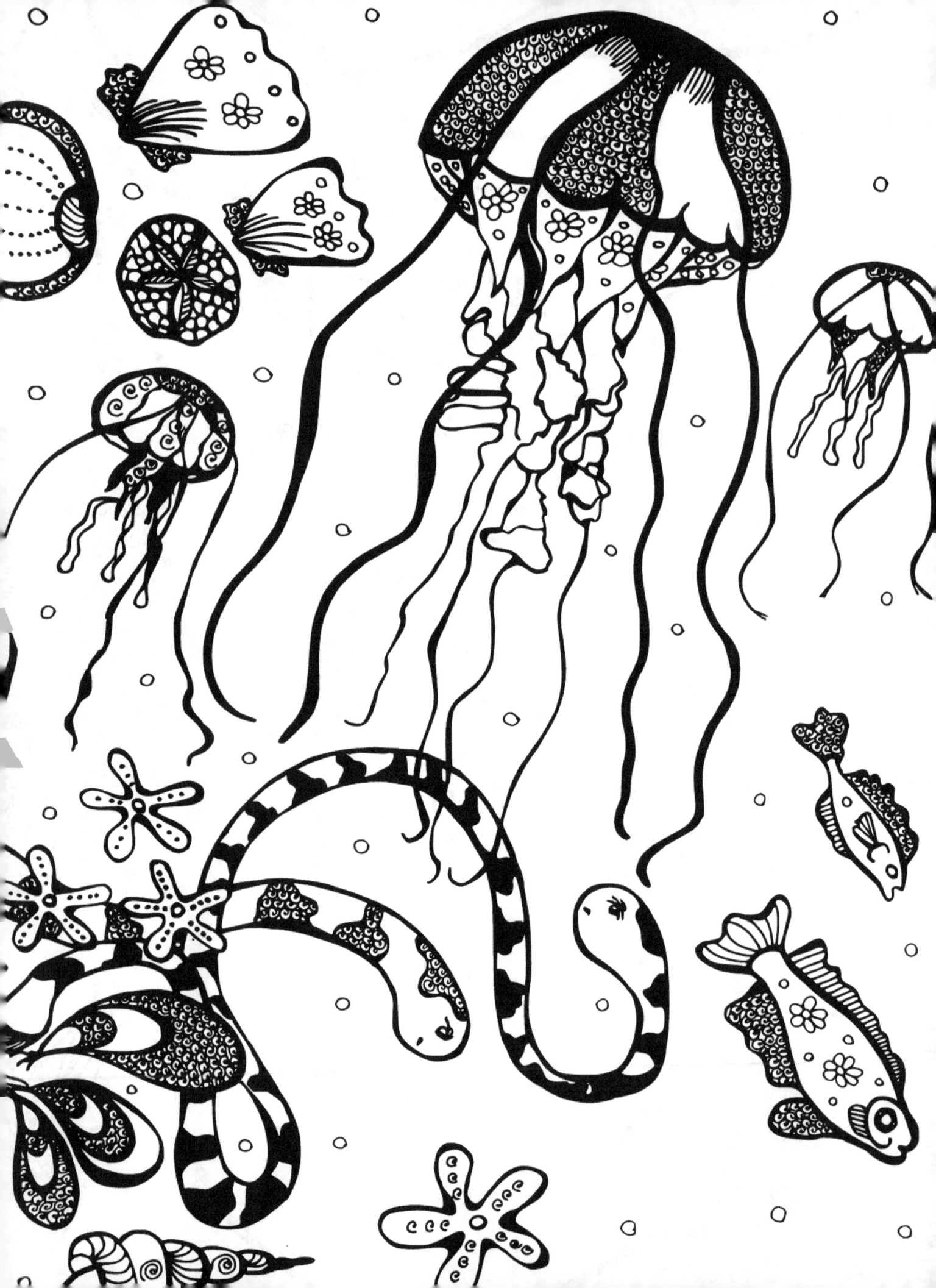

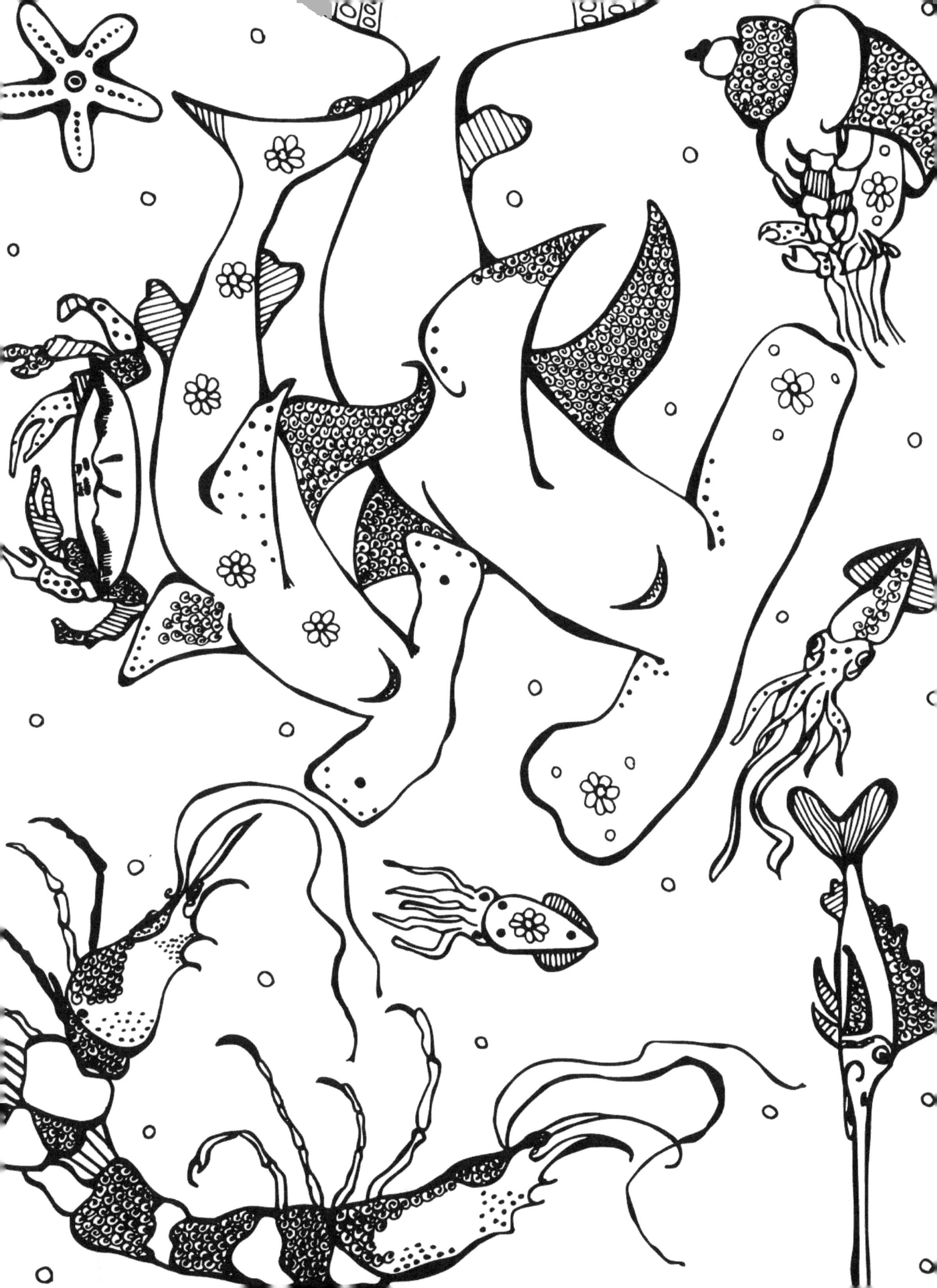

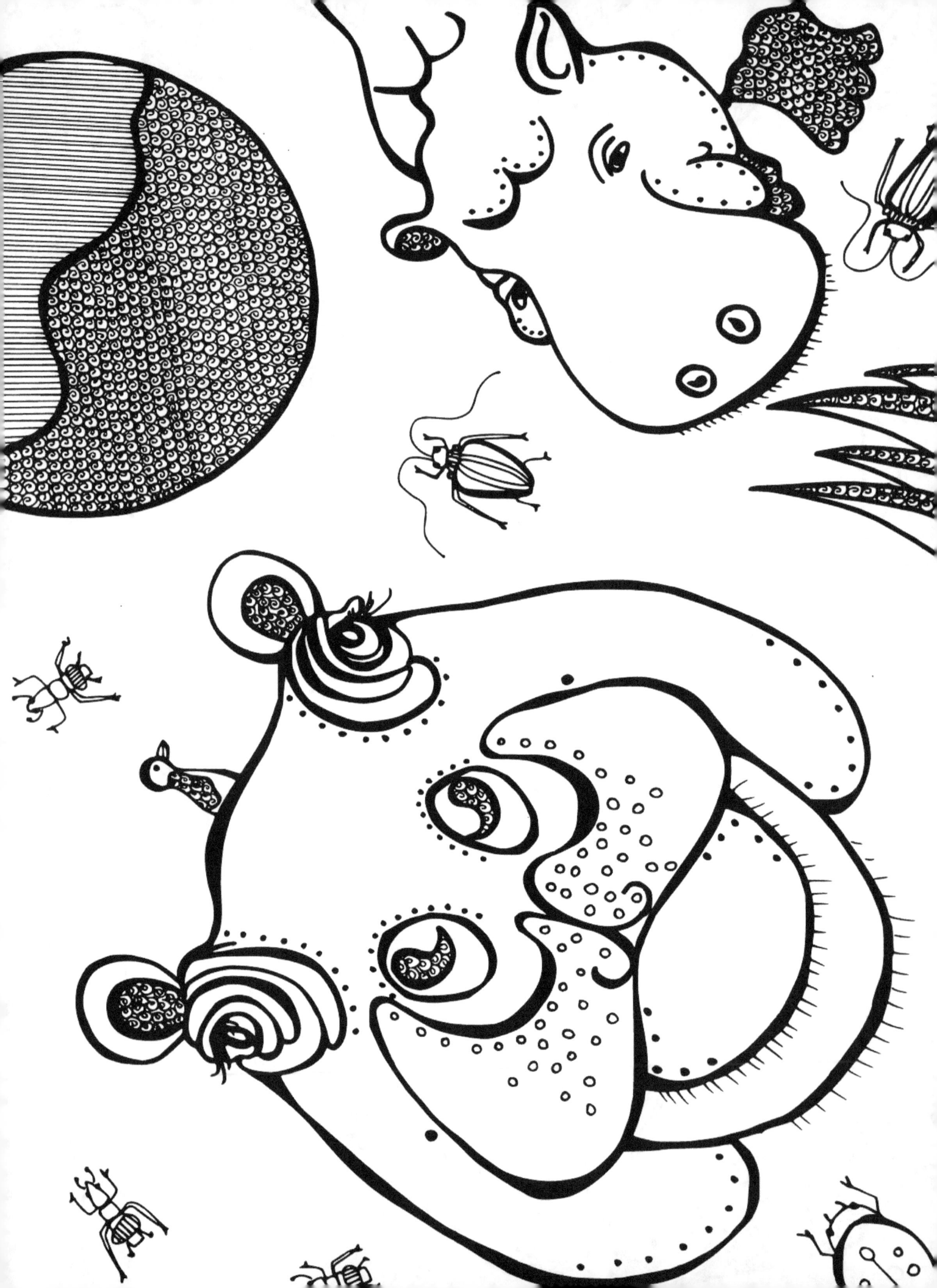

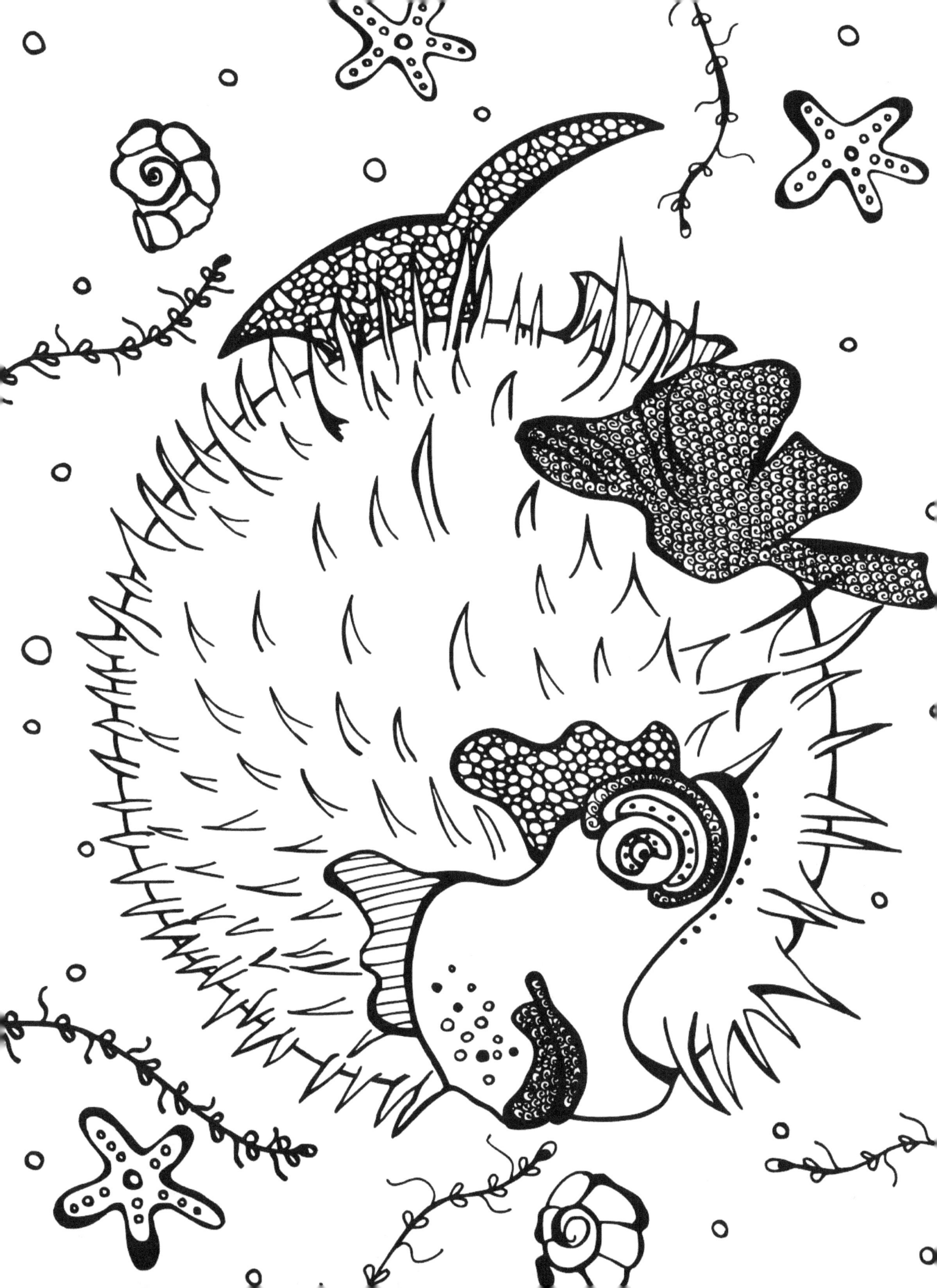

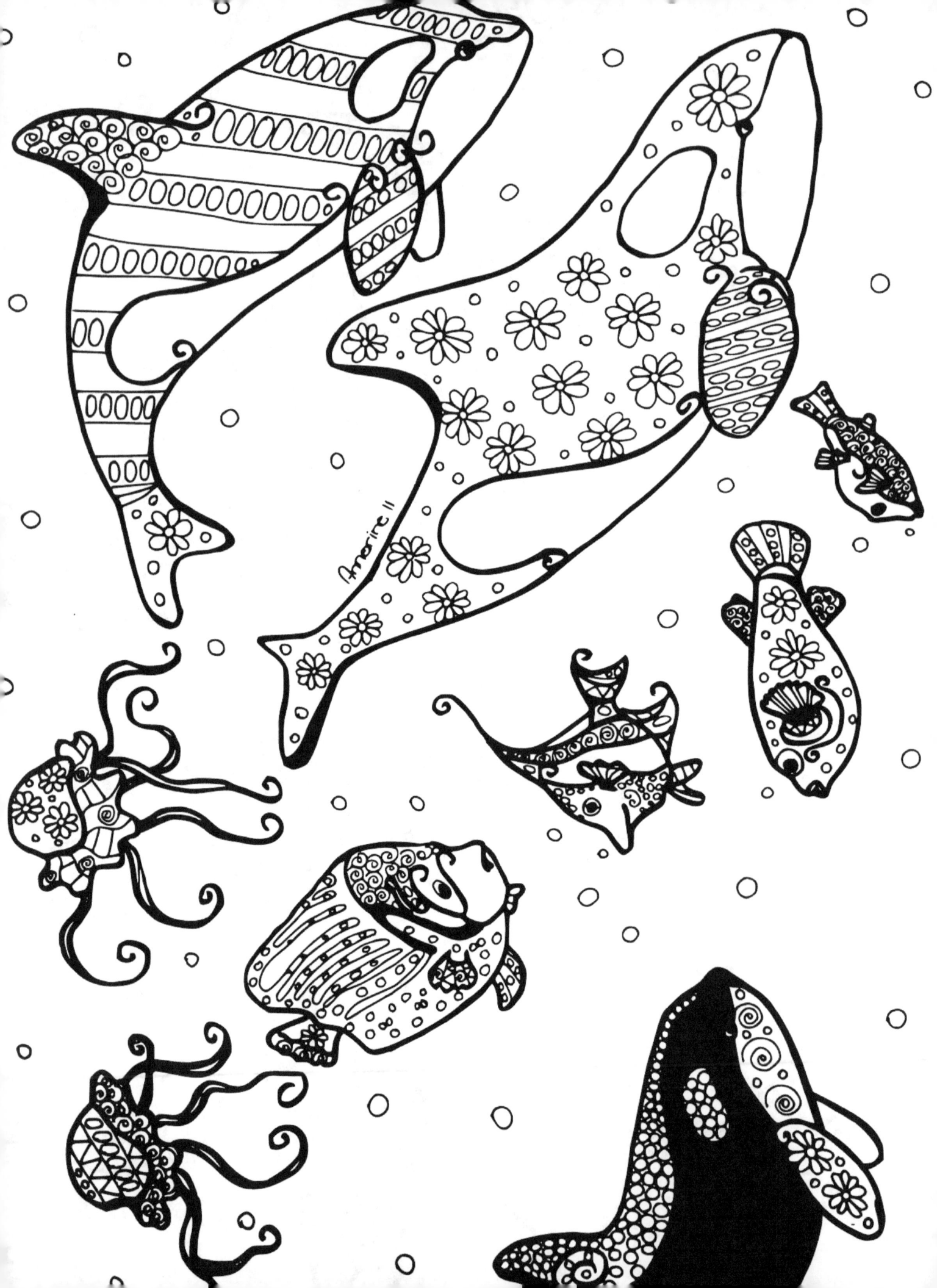

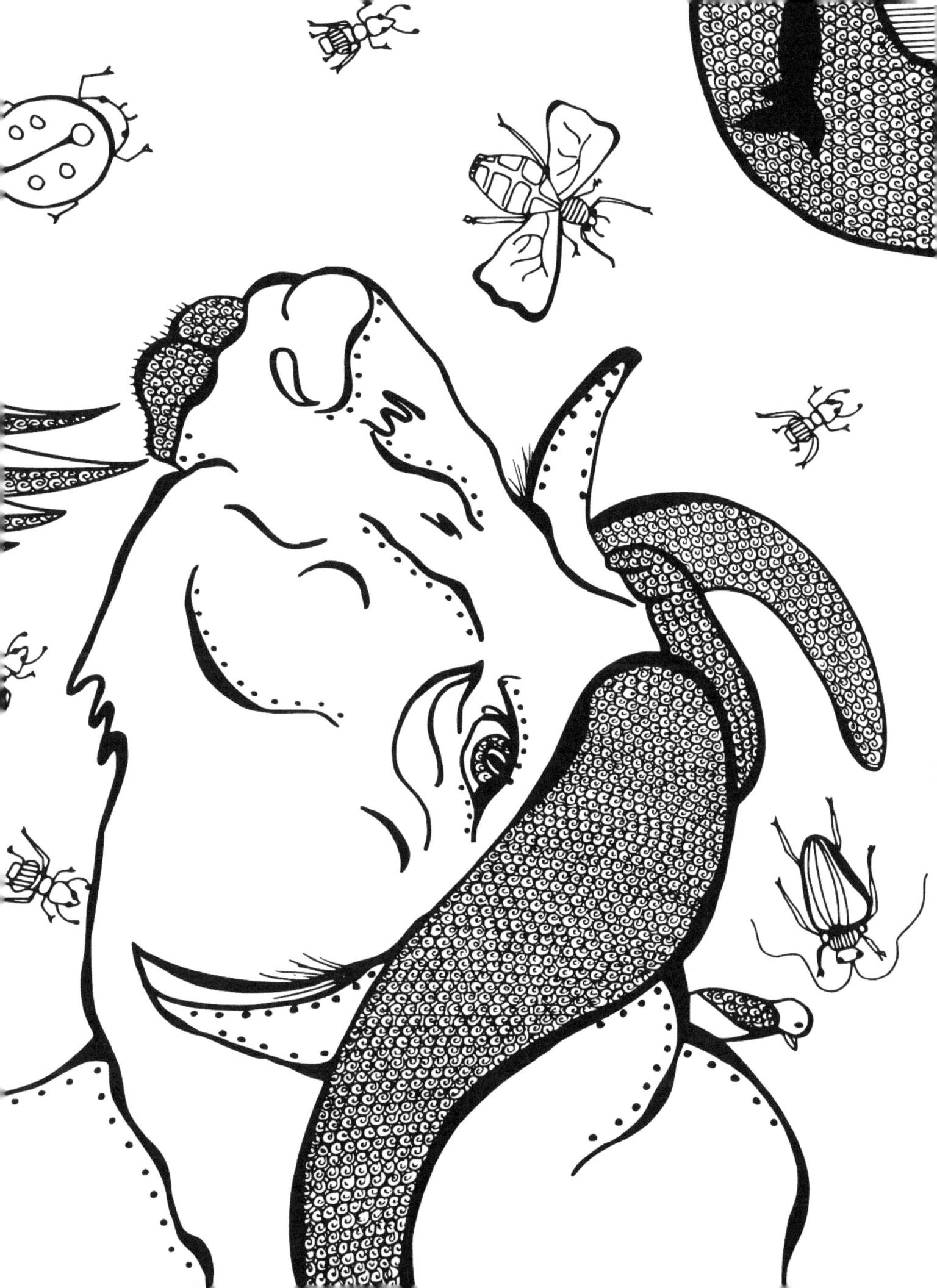

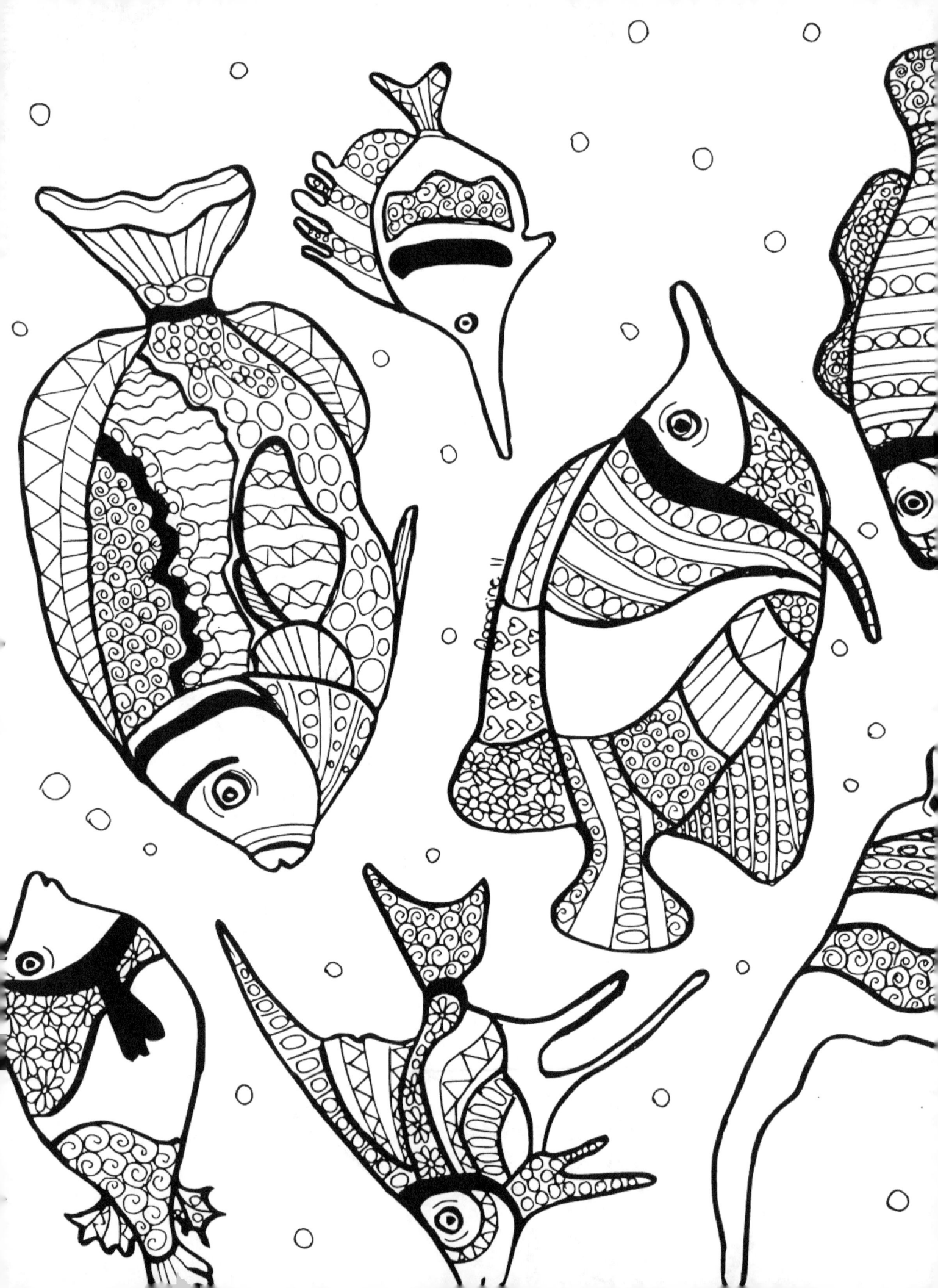

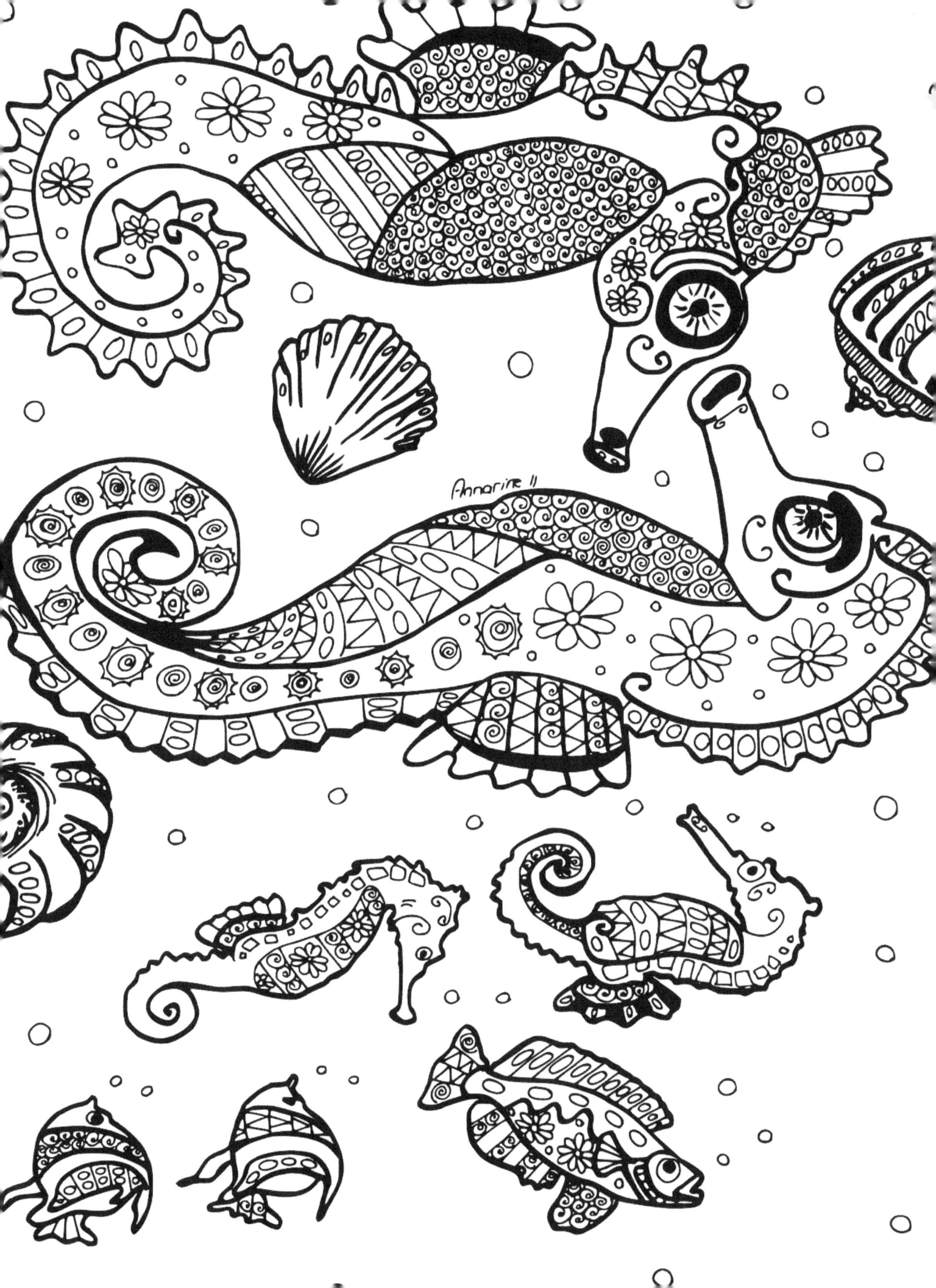

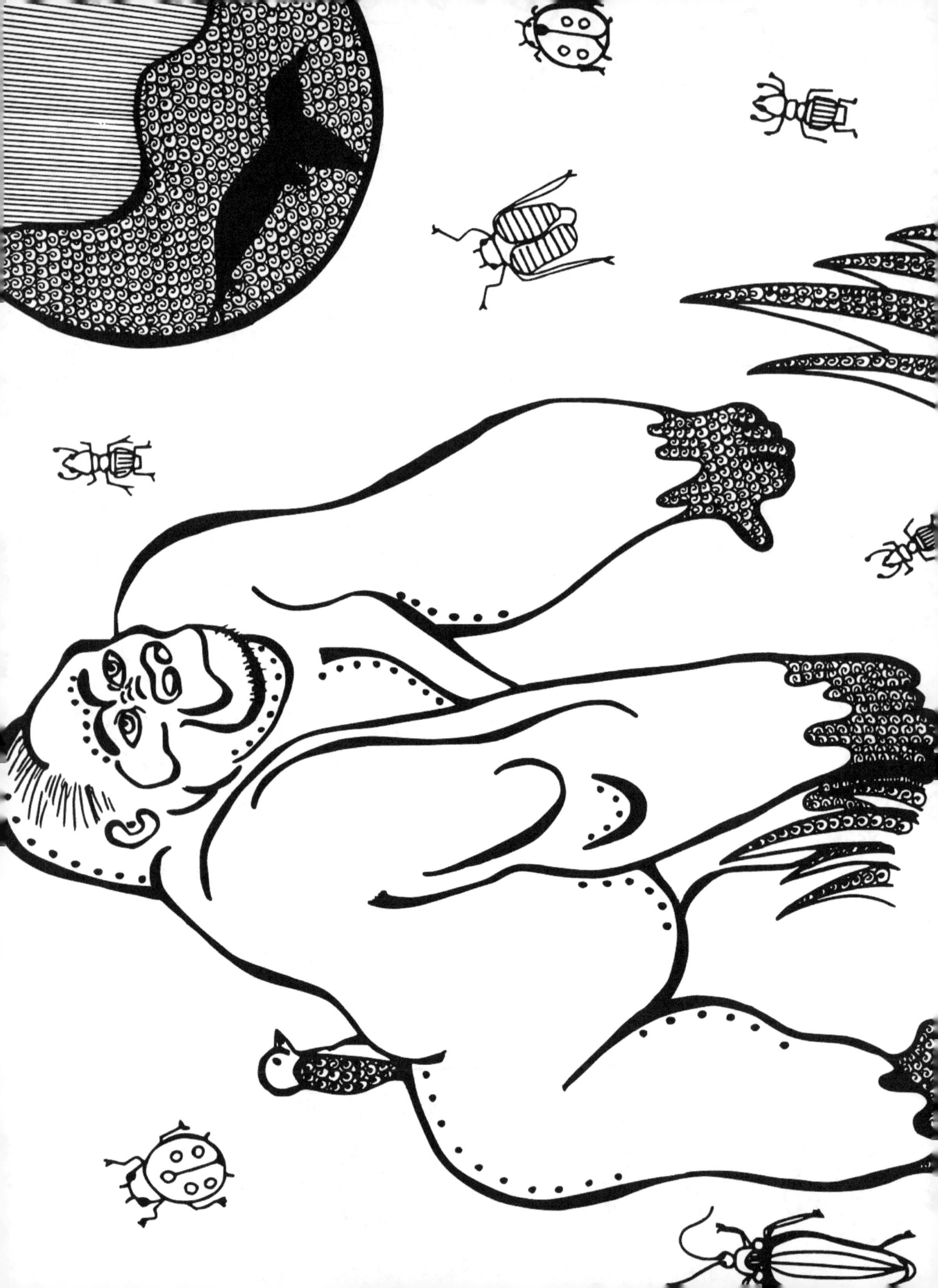

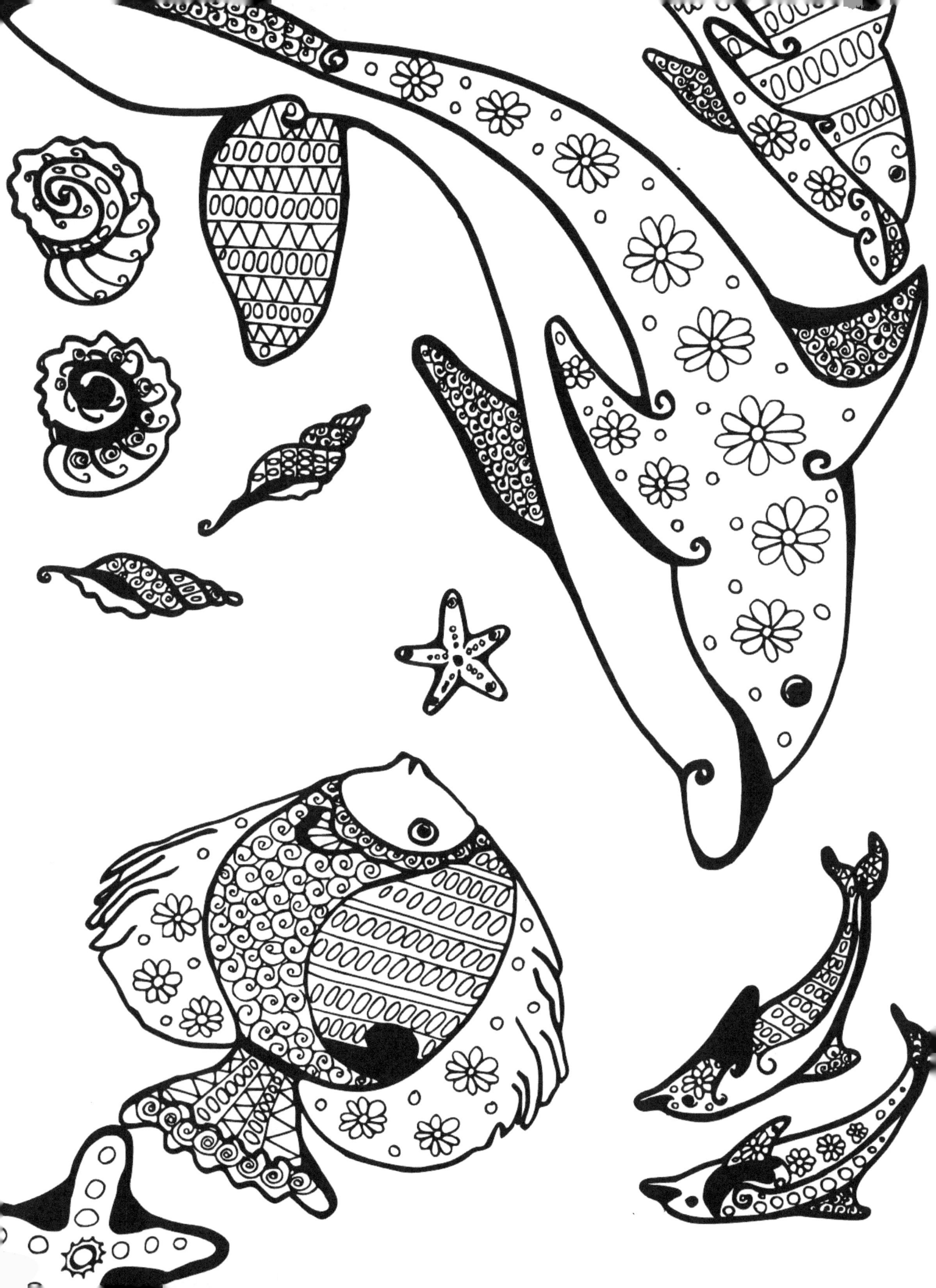

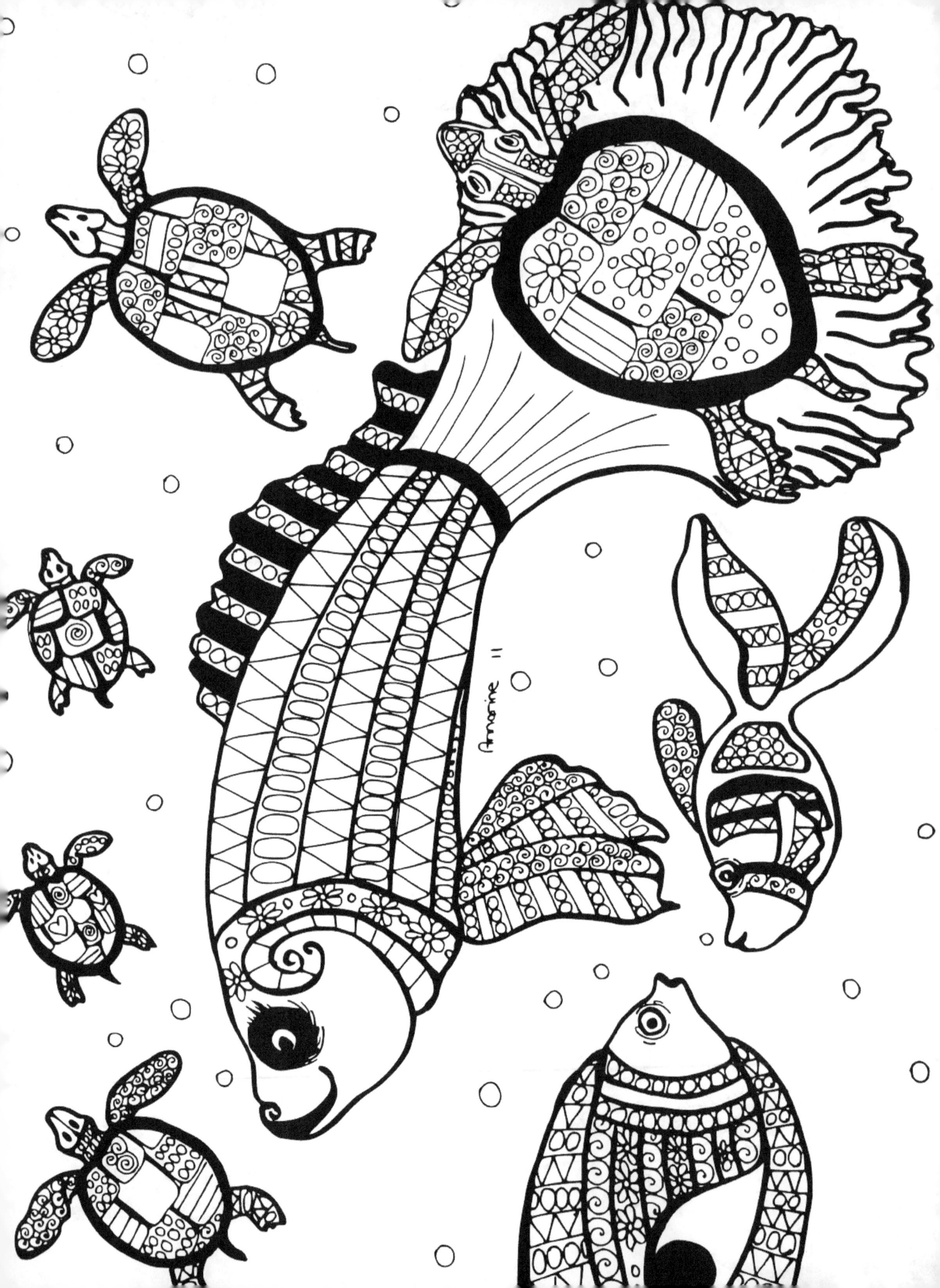

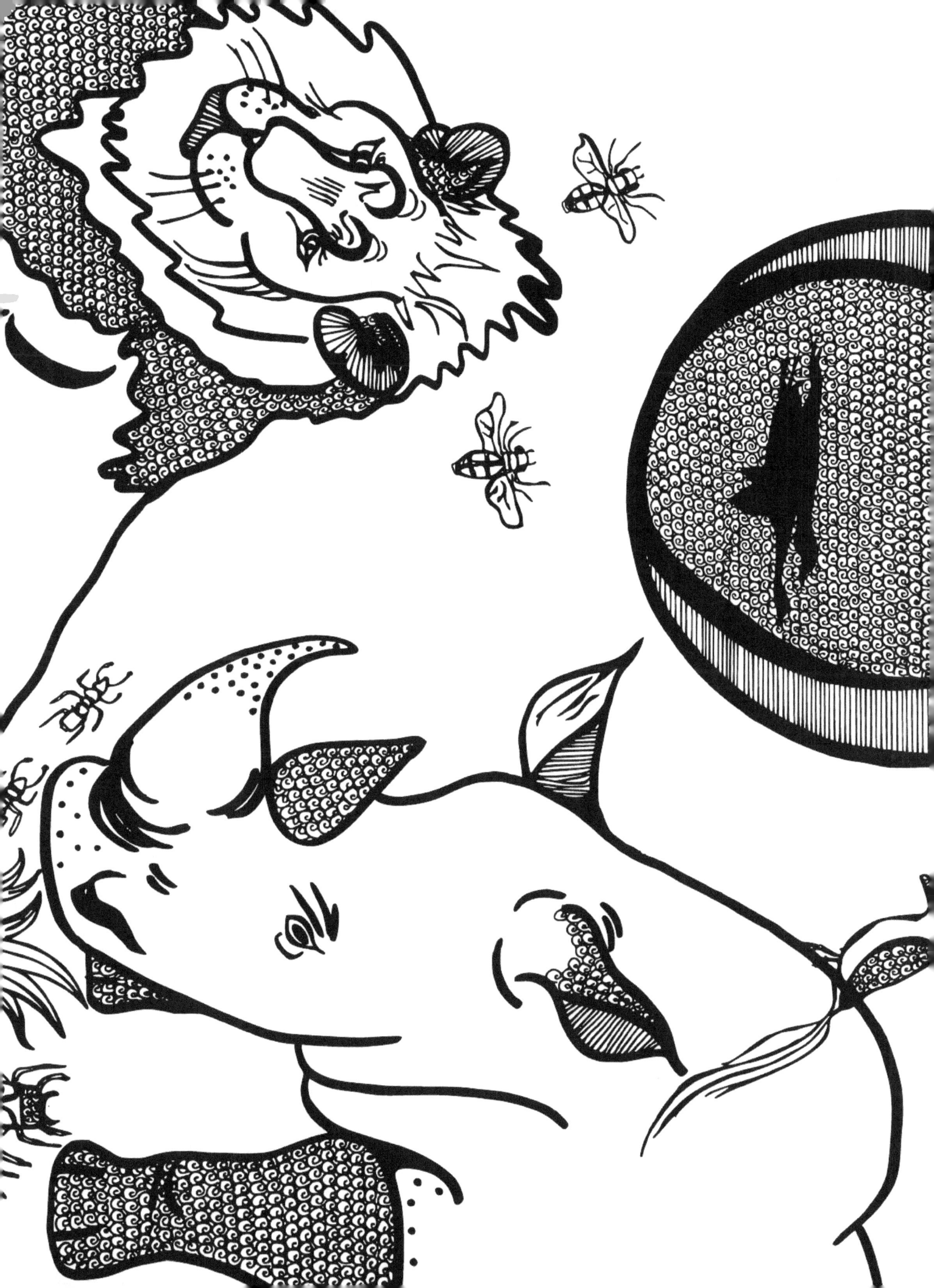

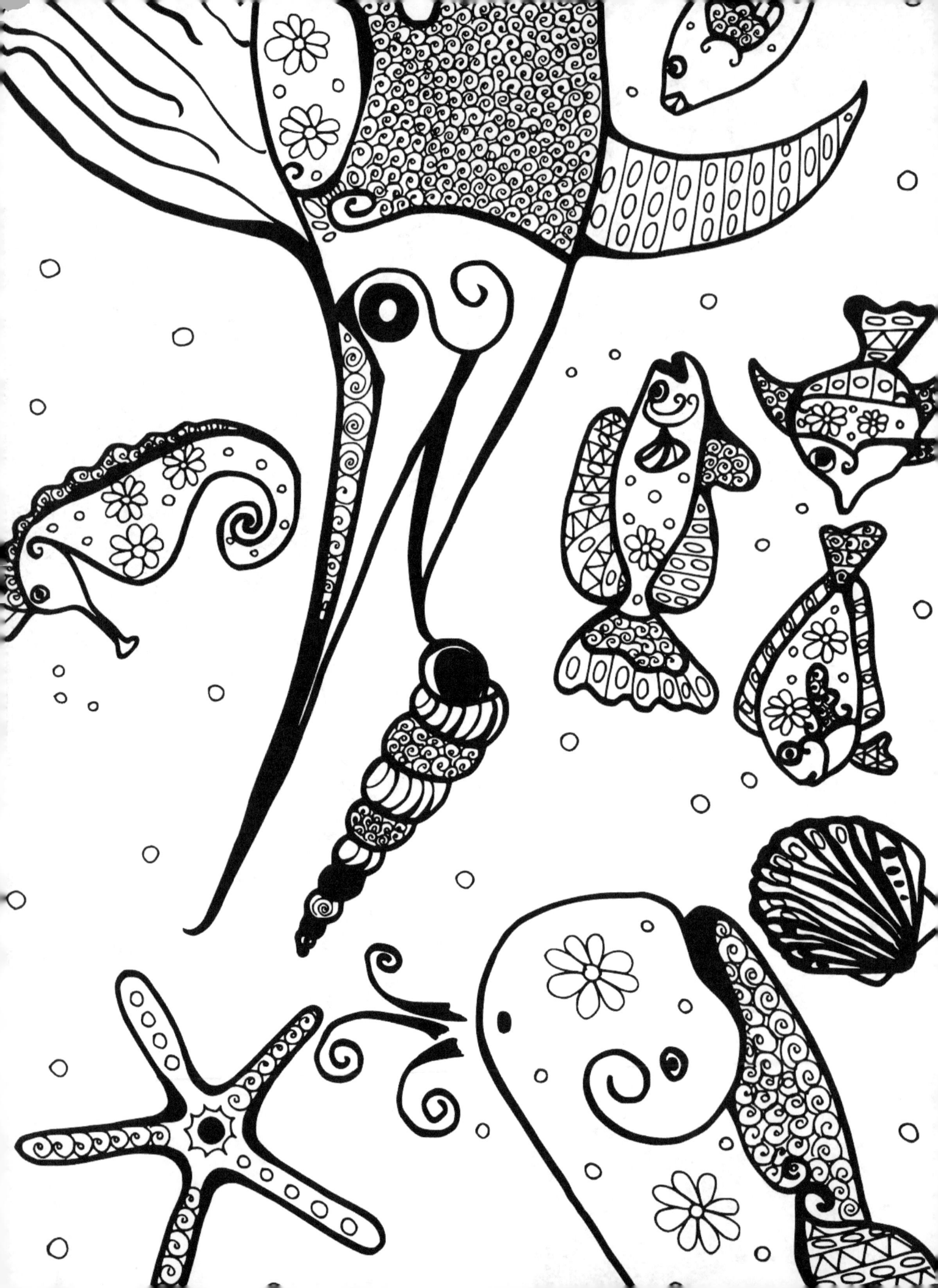

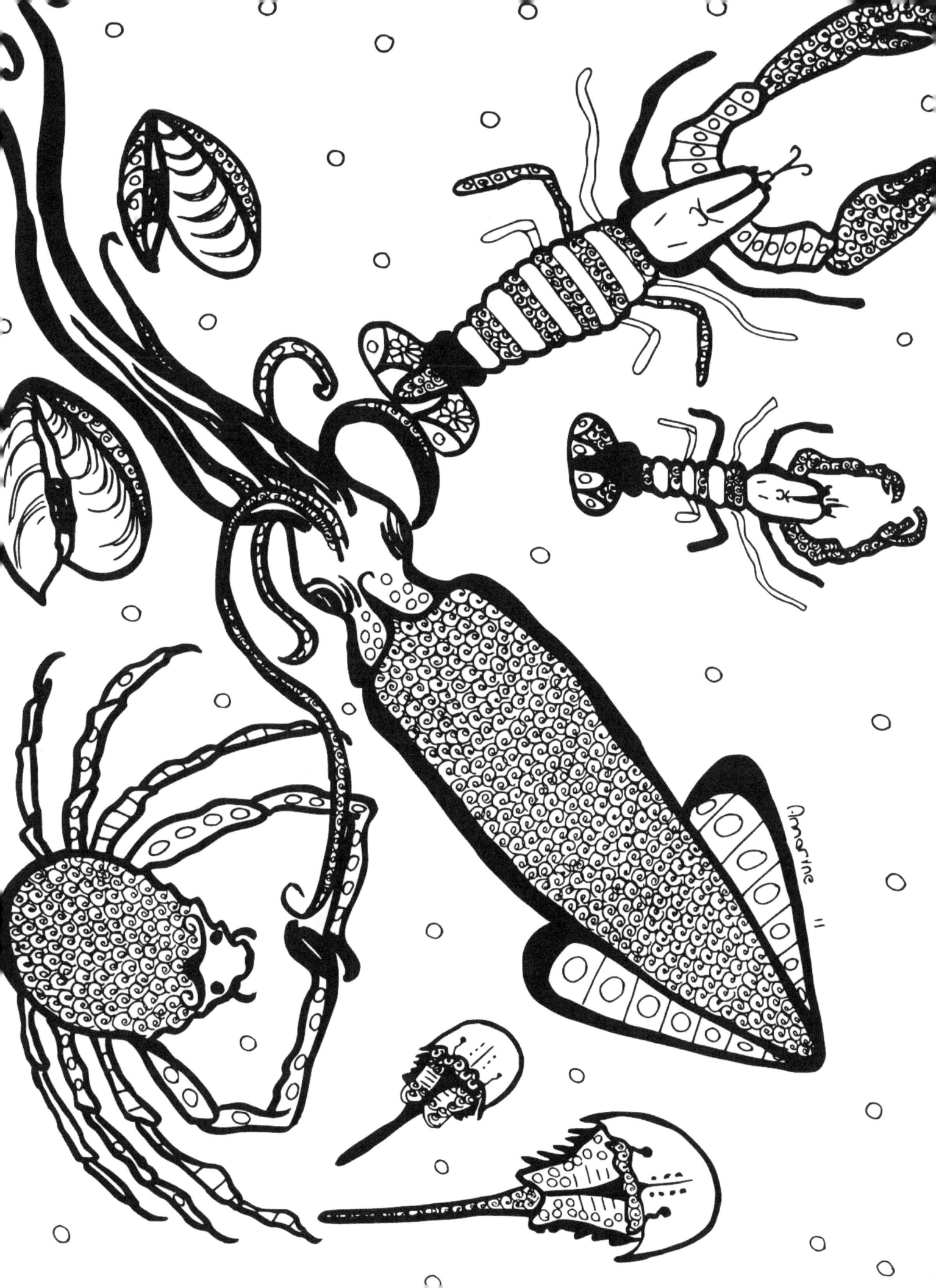

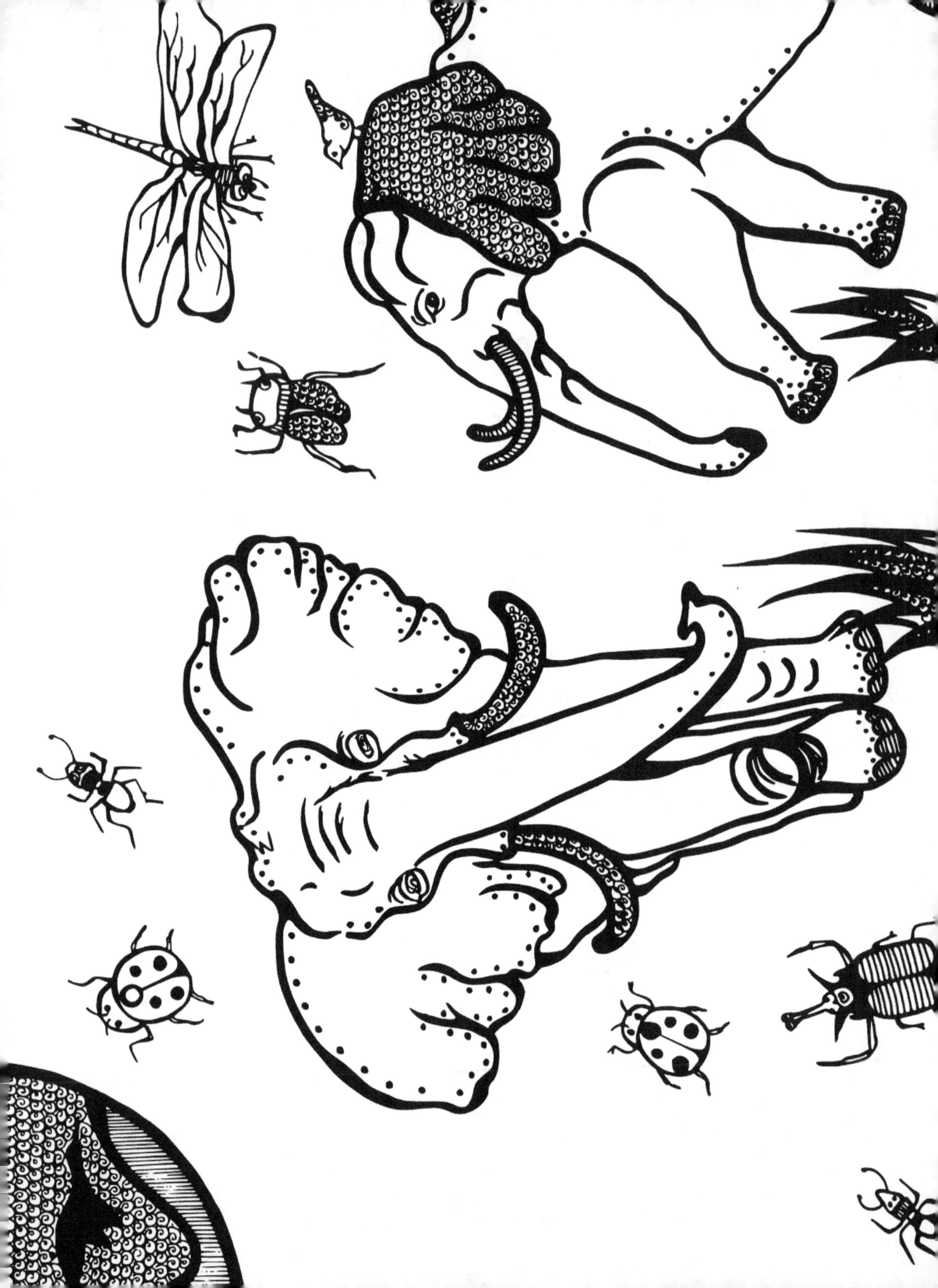

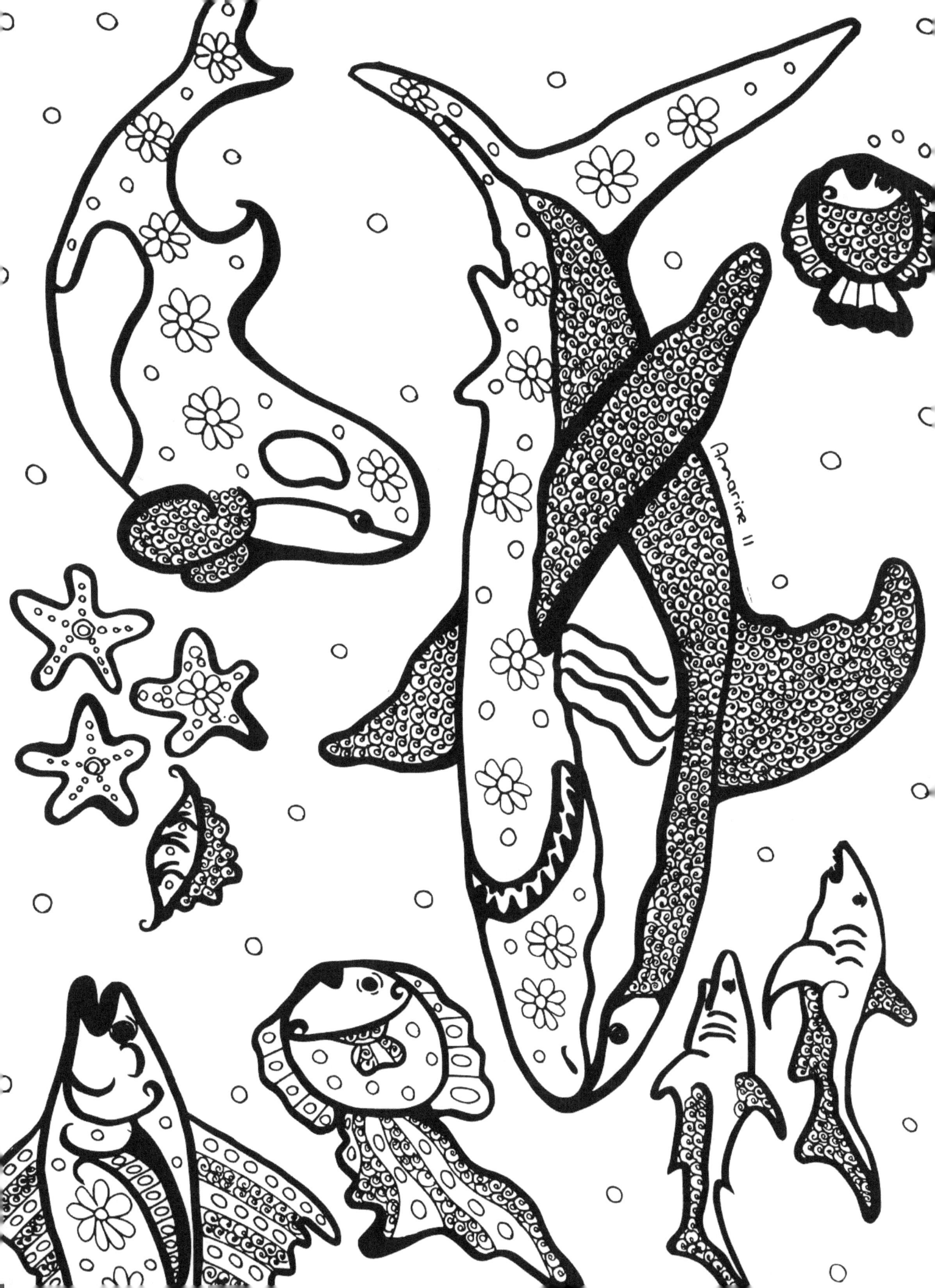

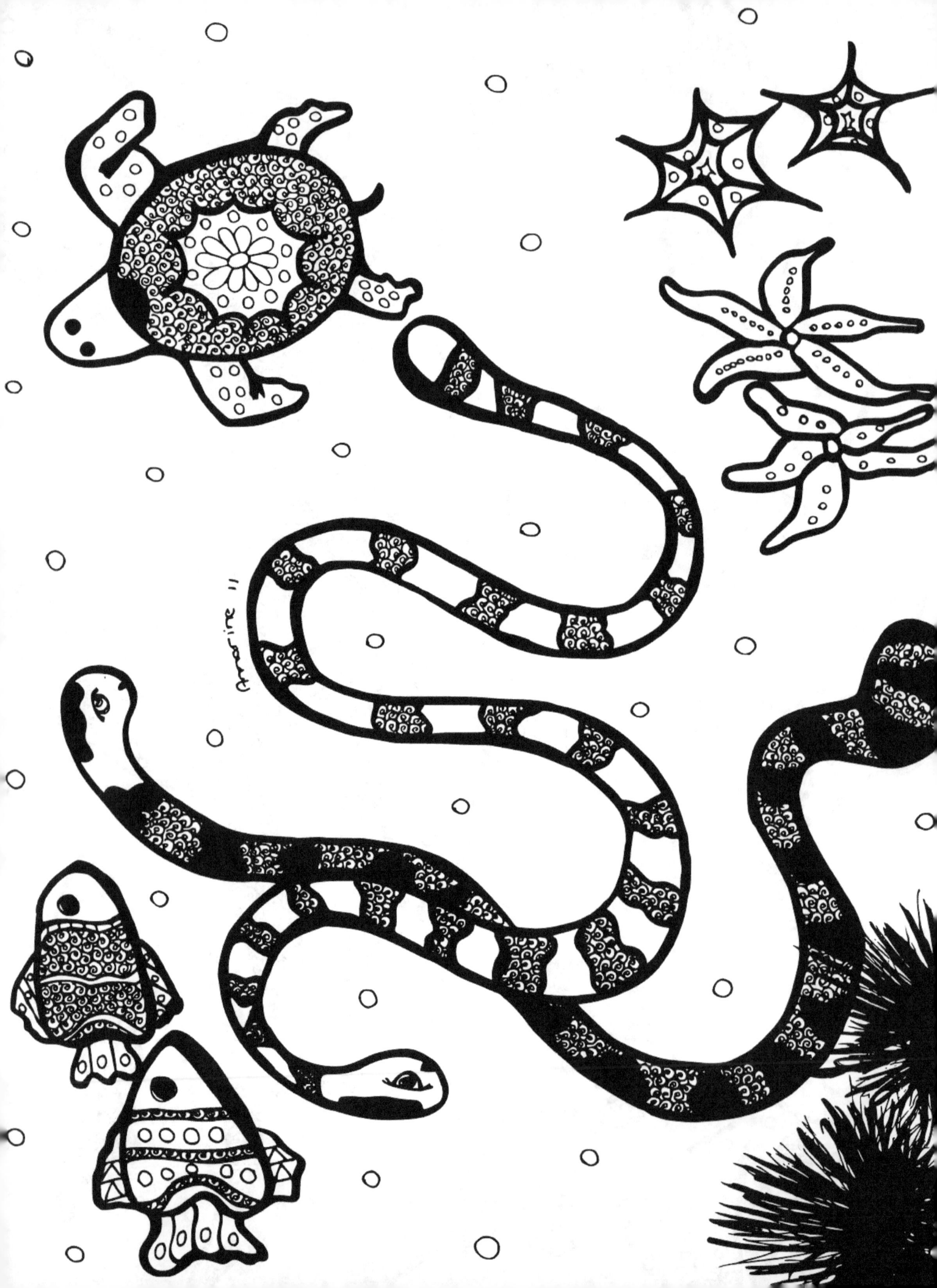

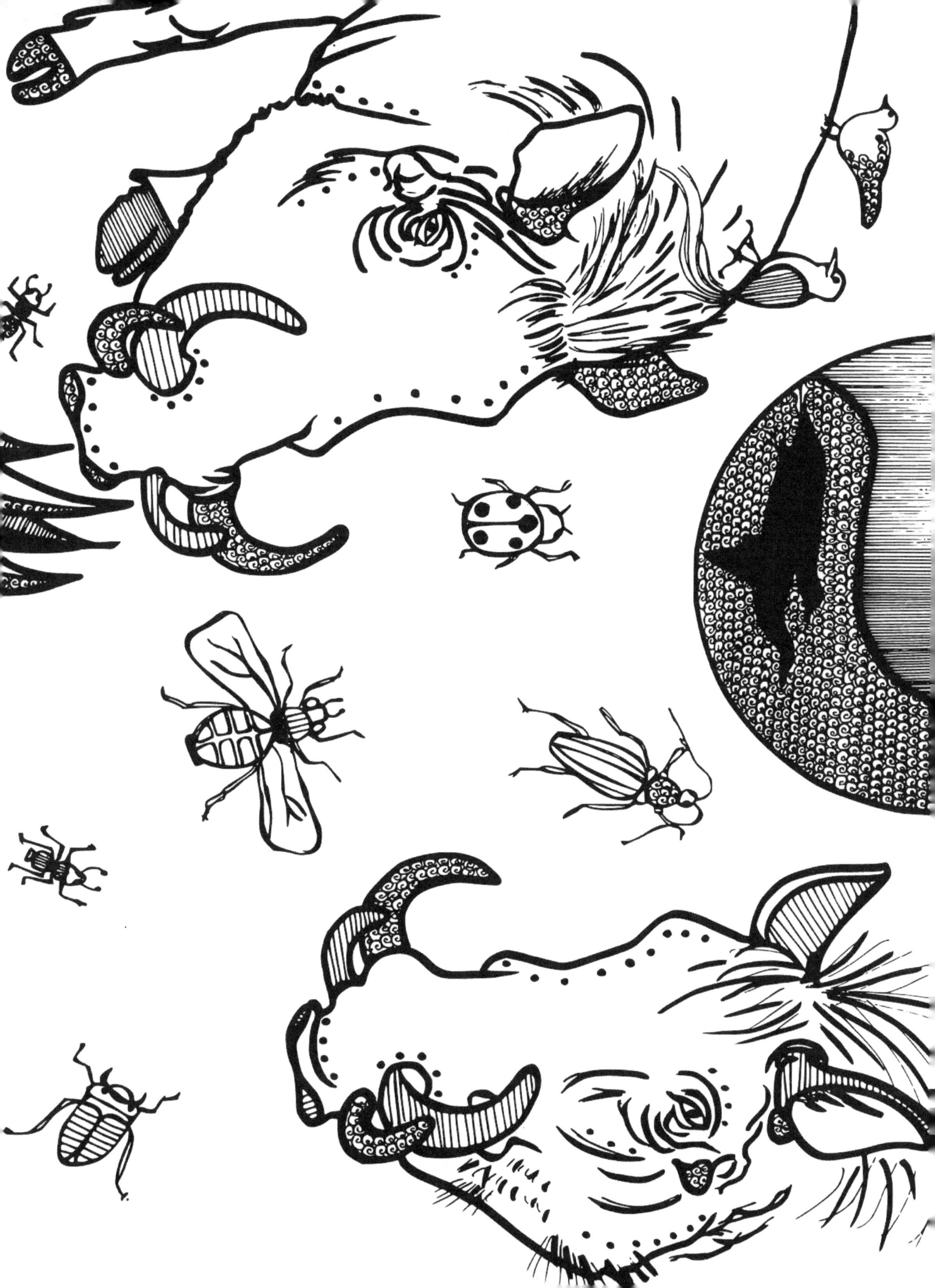

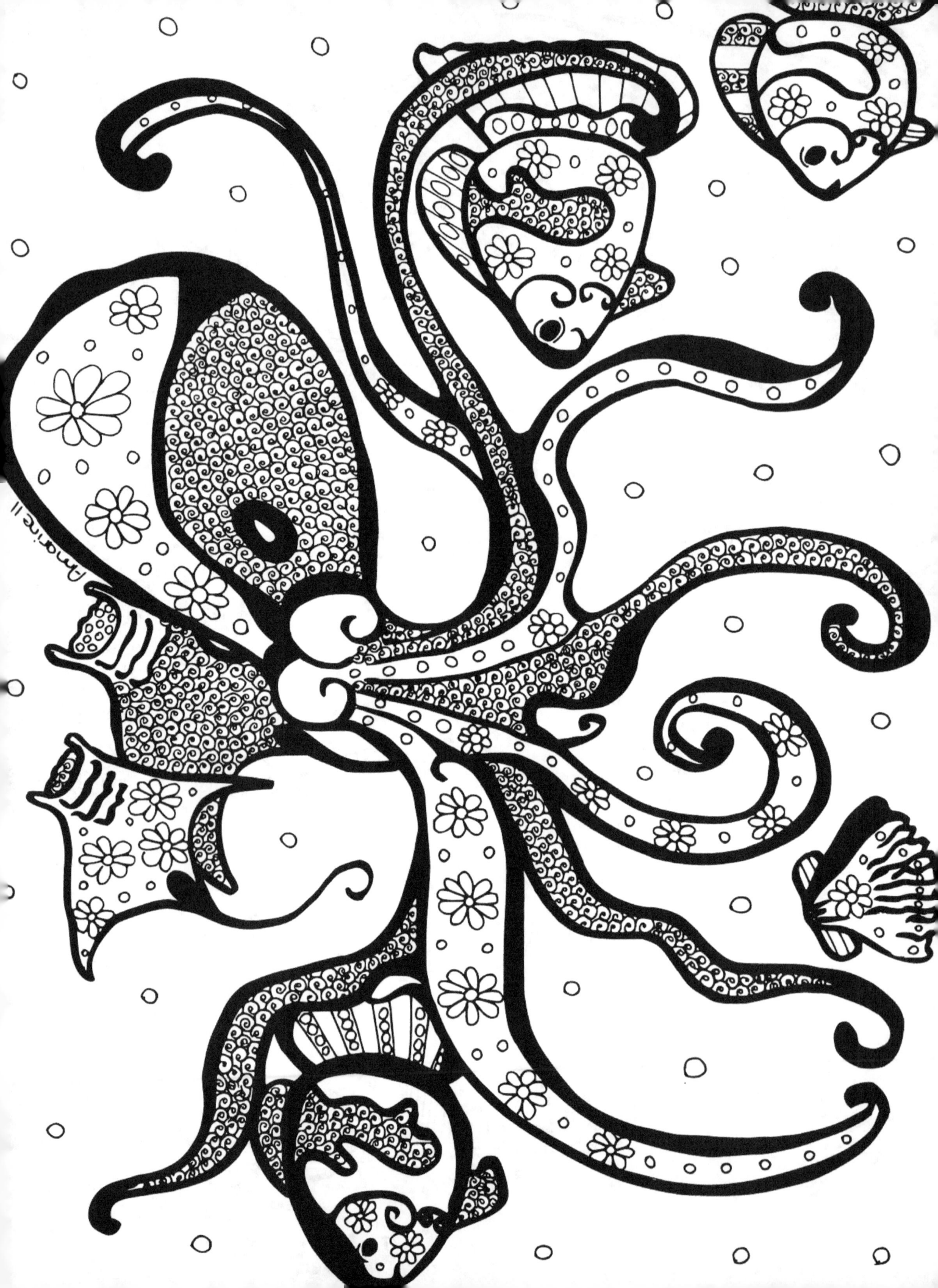

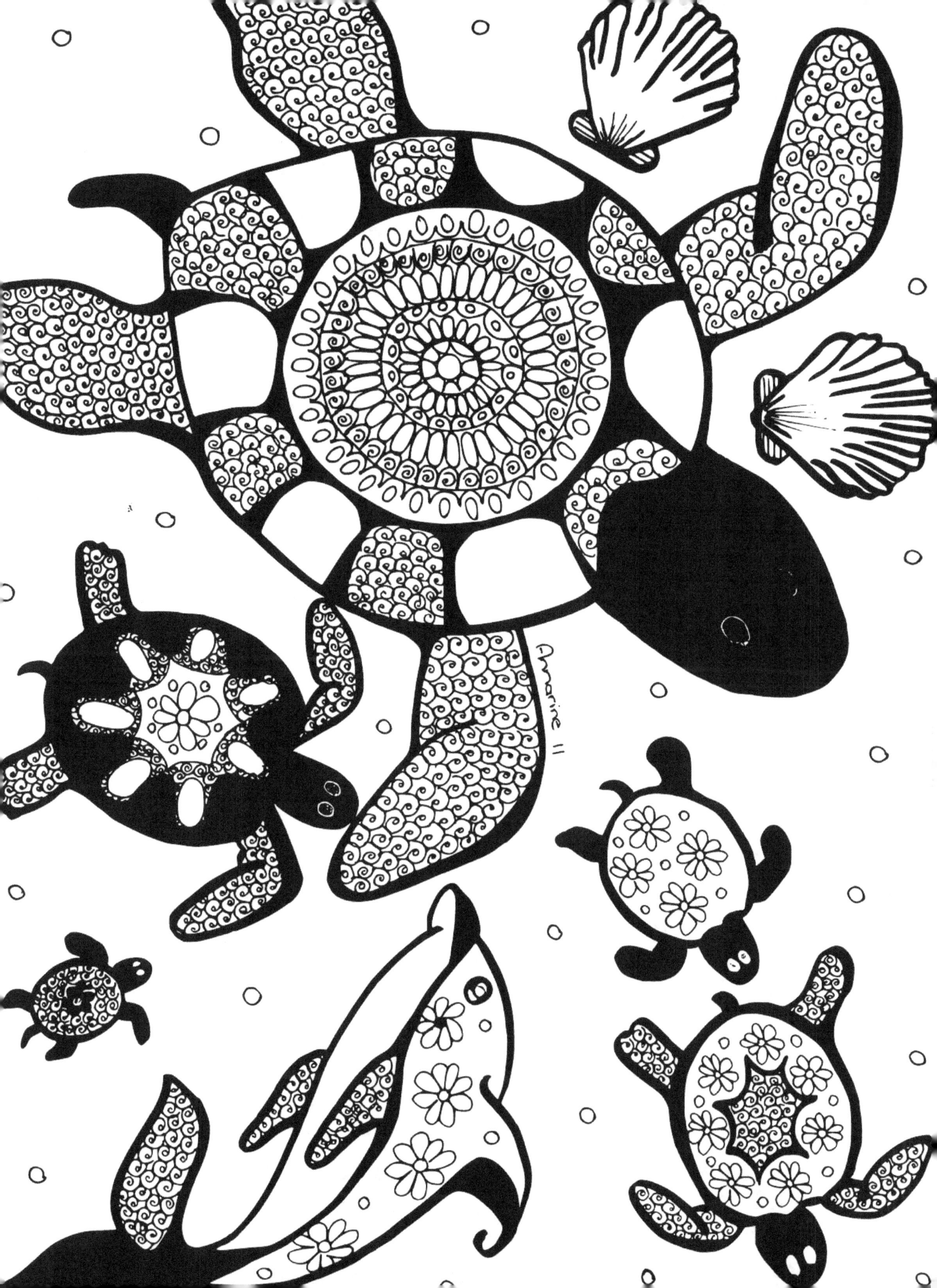

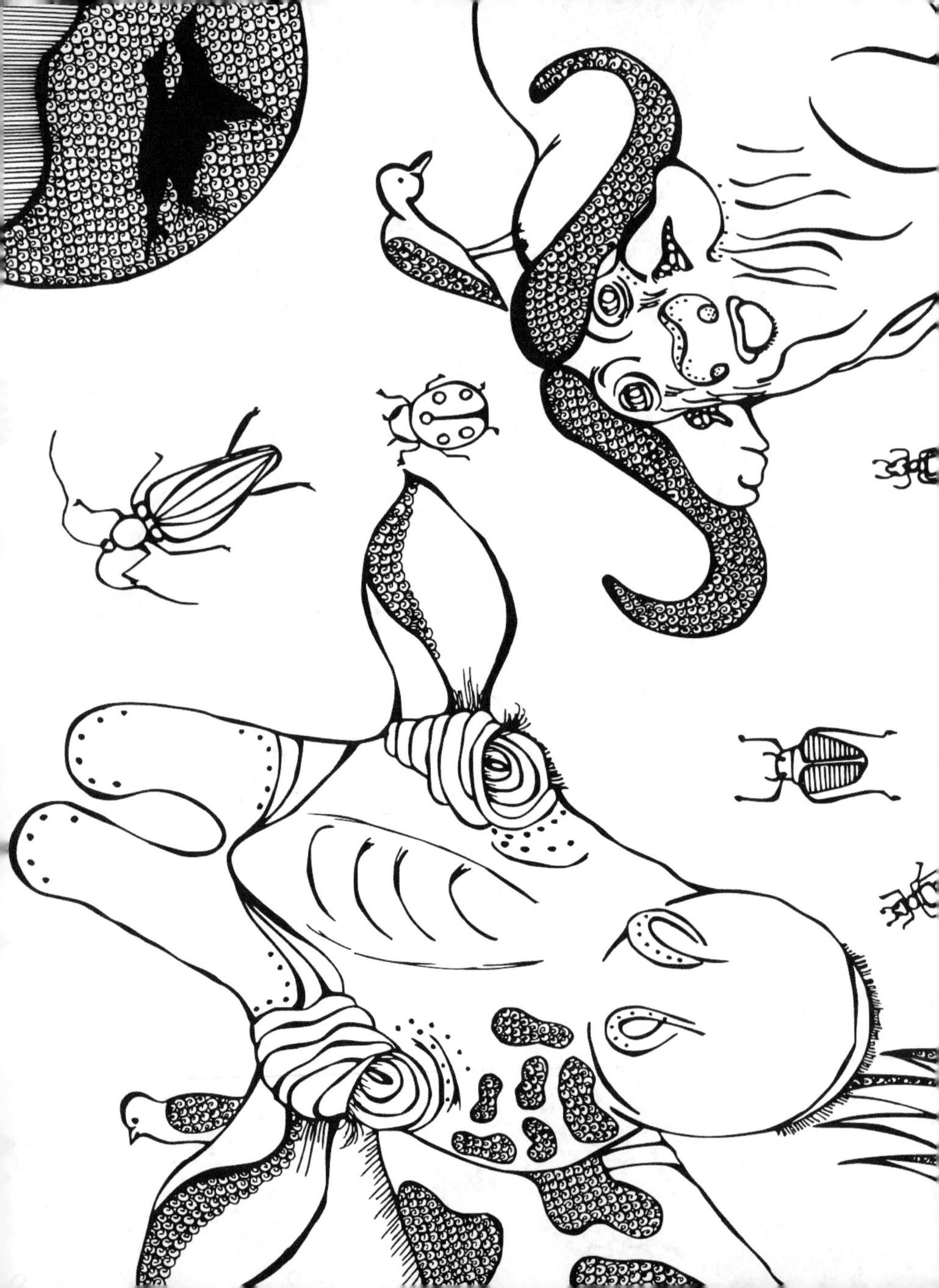

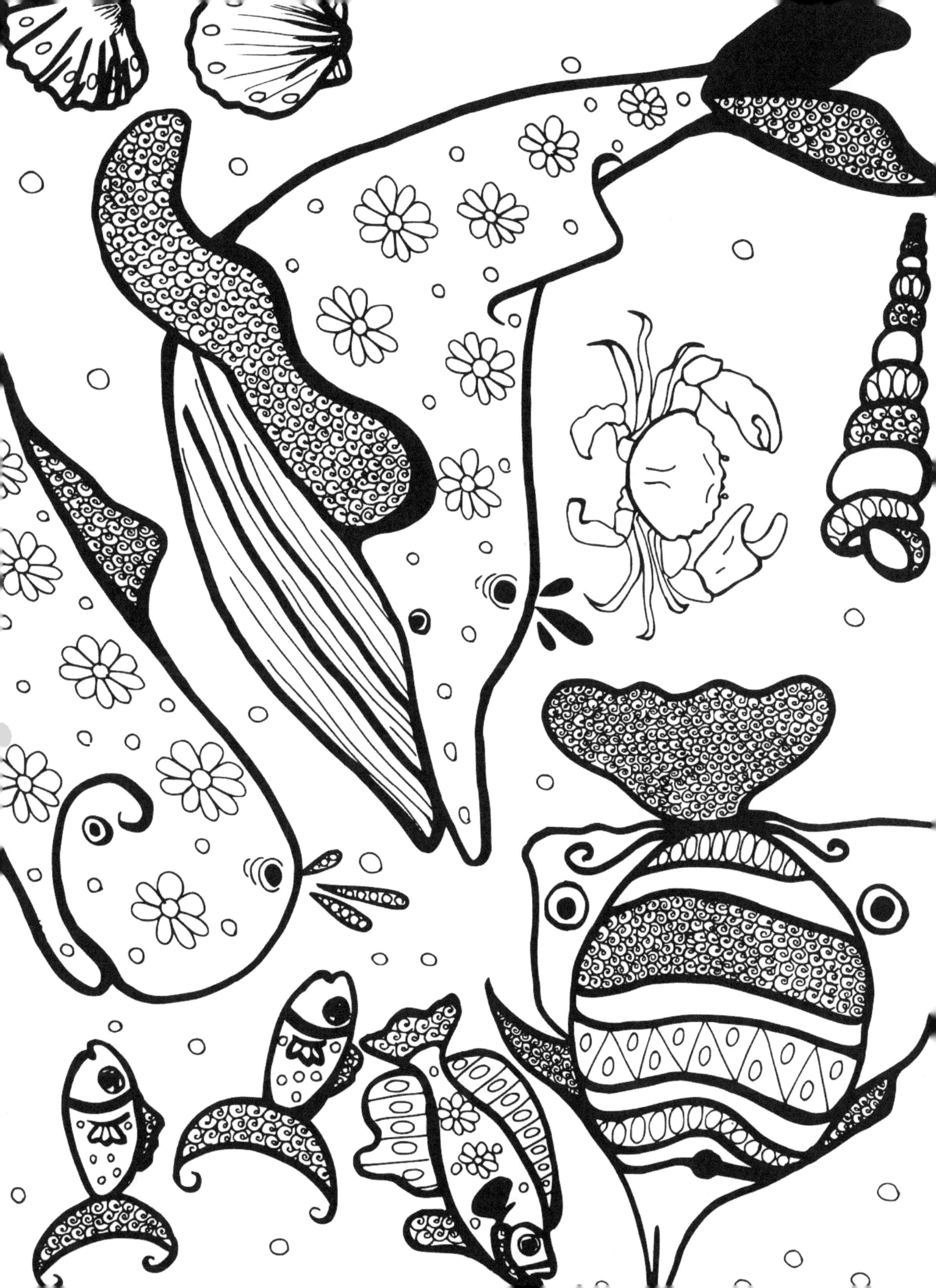

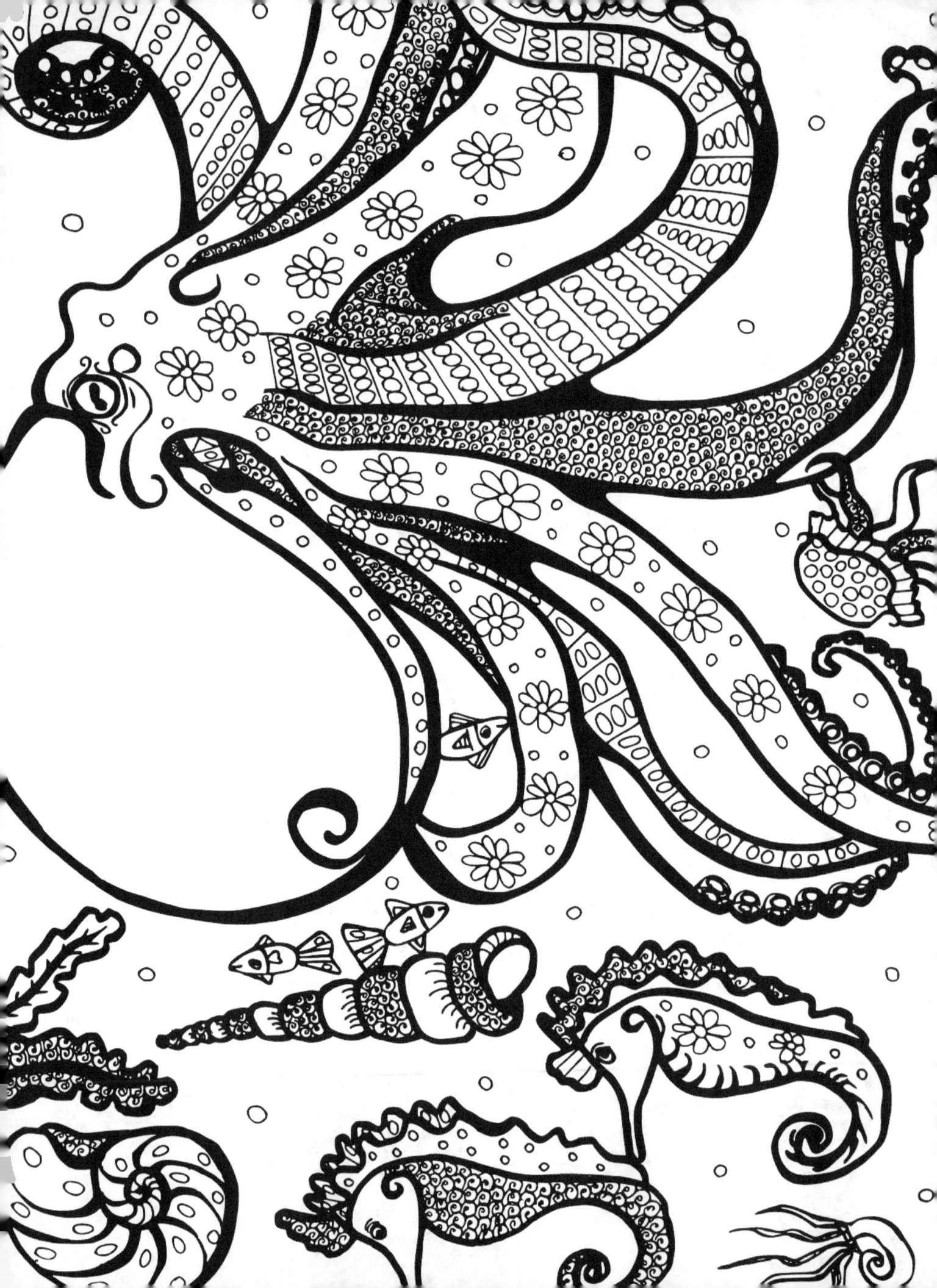

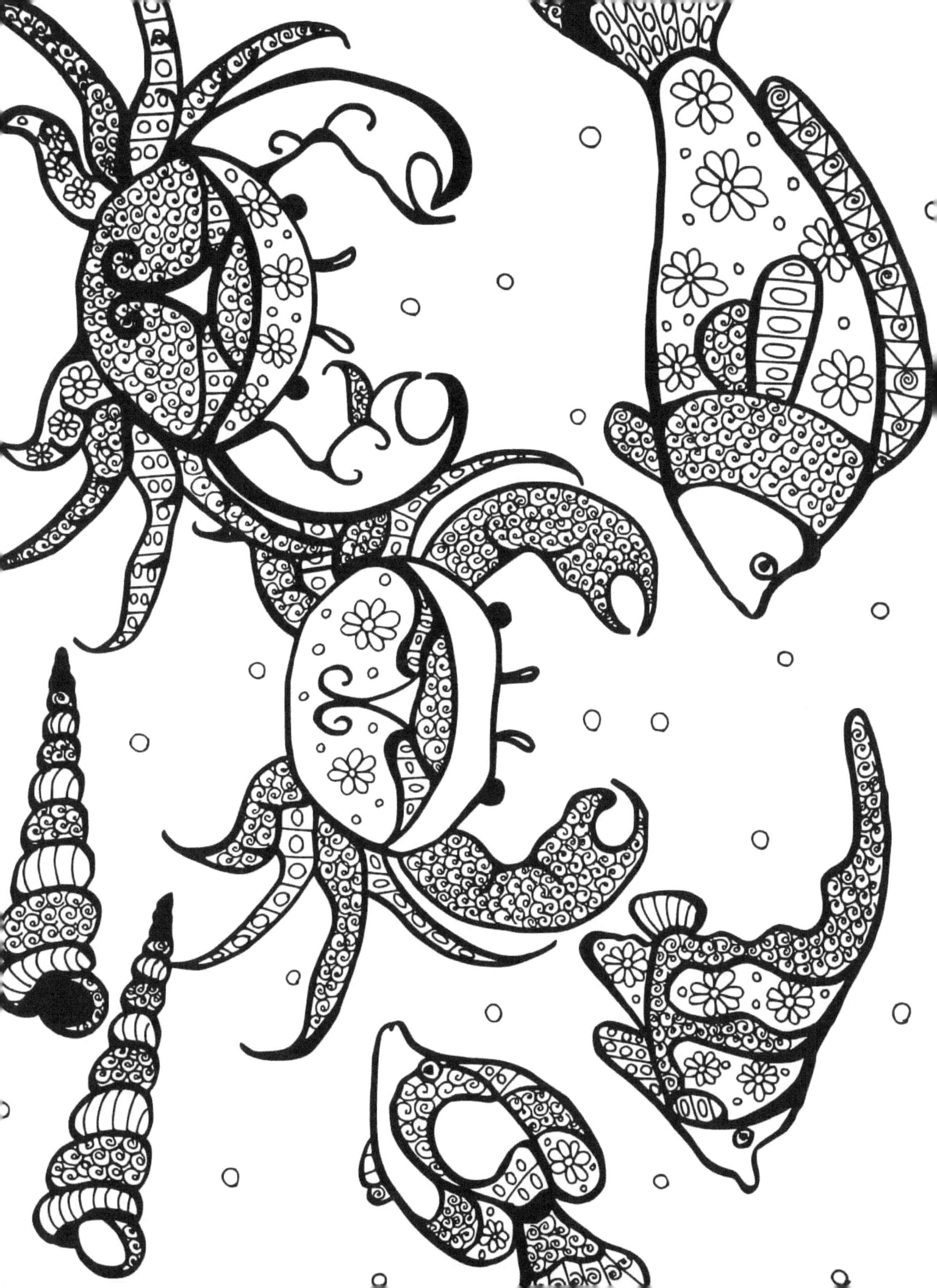